THE FIELD OF NONSENSE

The Field of Nonsense

ELIZABETH SEWELL

FOLCROFT LIBRARY EDITIONS / 1973

Library of Congress Cataloging in Publication Data

Sewell, Elizabeth, 1919-
   The field of nonsense.

   Reprint of the 1952 ed. published by Chatto
and Windus, London.
   Bibliography: p.
   1. English wit and humor--History and criticism.
I. Title.
[PR932.S4 1973]   827'.8'09   73-6991
ISBN 0-8414-7558-X (lib. bdg.)

Manufactured in the United States of America

The Field of Nonsense

ELIZABETH SEWELL

1952

CHATTO AND WINDUS

LONDON

PUBLISHED BY

Chatto and Windus

LONDON

*

Clarke, Irwin and Co. Ltd.

TORONTO

PRINTED BY

BUTLER AND TANNER LTD.

FROME AND LONDON

To a bountiful giver of twelve months' hospitality

THE OHIO STATE UNIVERSITY

Alma Mater indeed,
munificent both in kindness and in funds,
this book is dedicated by its author

(who hopes she made it plain that her journey to
Ohio State University to study Nonsense was no
reflection upon the high seriousness and purpose of
that vast, populous, lively, unexpected and beloved
Seat of Learning)

KEY TO ABBREVIATIONS
OF PRINCIPAL WORKS

*

LEWIS CARROLL

Alice's Adventures in Wonderland, 1865	A.A.W.
Through the Looking-Glass, 1872	T.L.G.
The Hunting of the Snark, 1876	H.S.
Sylvie and Bruno, 1889	S.B.
Sylvie and Bruno Concluded, 1893	S.B.C.

EDWARD LEAR

A Book of Nonsense, 1846	B.N.
Nonsense Songs, Stories, Botany and Alphabets, 1871	N.S.B.
More Nonsense Pictures, Rhymes, Botany, etc., 1872	M.N.
Laughable Lyrics, A Fourth Book of Nonsense Poems, Songs, Botany, Music, etc., 1877	L.L.
Nonsense Songs and Stories (Posthumous), 1895	N.S.S.

CONTENTS

*

Chapter	Page
1 Sense and Nonsense	1
2 A Double Rule of Three	7
3 The Right Words	17
4 Word Play and Dialectic	27
5 One and One and One and One and One	44
6 Concrete and Fastidious	55
7 Cats, Coffee, and Thirty-Times-Three	61
8 Seven Maids with Seven Mops	81
9 Bats and Tea-Trays	97
10 The Balance of Brillig	115
11 Cunning Old Fury	130
12 'The Heart is Affected'	149
13 'Dodgfather, Dodgson & Coo'	163
14 Will You, Won't You?	183
Bibliography	195

They built their fortune with a pack of cards,
A tower of cards, breathless scaffolding of chance;
They built their tower to make the stars dance
A tiptoe on its parapet,
Heel and toe they were to go
In Babylon along the crenellations
To old priests' incantations.
Very haughty these were, but at their prayer
The stars might leave their shoes on the topmost stair—
But the stars burst their shoestrings, and all their feet were bare,
Dancing their pattern to the tune the old cards were calling,
(King and Emperor and Pope)
Handled hieratically, a horoscope,
Centuried games of patience, the zodiac falling
Into constellated suits of red and black,
Until God smote them with the coming of day, lime-green and heliotrope,
And all the pack went whirling
Into a wounded sky,
Sandstorm of emblems, sky-cloud lightened and thundered,
And God sundered them in the cold of the morning air
And the majesty of their mouths moving.

The stars put on their shoes,
Soberly disposed;
Cock crows
Dimpling above the broken stone-yards
Where dirty folk yawn and stretch their elbows;
But we hold back the dawn
Hours upon hours,
Three score years or three score miles and ten,
By candlelight dancing our way to broken towers
With little candles our swirling twirling skirts have blown about,
And in our dance of words the stars pop in and out,
And God smiles sleepily, and you see Him reach
His Hand—for what? but already the stars have lost their track,
And farandole to our rigmarole,

For in my pocket I have that ancient pack,
(King and Emperor and Pope)
And dance for ever on Babylon's plain,
In tight star-figures, shuffling the cards of speech
In a mountebank brain,
Fearing demoniac powers,
But in celestial hope
To wind God back into the dance again.

Chapter 1

SENSE AND NONSENSE

NONSENSE IS a term which appears in a great many contexts. It may be used by logicians to describe some contradiction in a system, by scientists to describe statements which supposedly do not tally with the known facts, by modern philosophers to describe sentences which seem to them to depart from the rules for making sense in the use of language. Ordinary people use the word 'Nonsense' in connection with situations or statements which do not conform to the facts as they are generally held to be, or which, more simply, are taken to be untrue. In every case, the one who employs the word must suppose that he or she knows what sense is, the opposite of which may be called nonsense, frequently with a not unenjoyable feeling of irritation.

To take up some such position, making a stand upon some particular ground and saying, 'This is sense, that is nonsense,' seems a comparatively simple thing to do, as a child draws a circle on the ground with a stick and says, 'This is Tom Tiddler's ground.' But it is not really simple at all, for the respective spheres of sense and nonsense cannot be mapped out in terms of spheres of influence, as if a line could be drawn on the map of thought separating the one from the other. The assumption that you know what sense is, and consequently what nonsense is, depends not on the acceptance or rejection of blocs of fact but upon the adoption of certain sets of mental relations. Whatever holds together according to these relationships will be sense, whatever does not will be nonsense.

The special people just mentioned, the logician, the scientists and so on, will illustrate the point. Take the logician first. He employs a system of mental relations which has a total intolerance of whatever does not fit in with it. In logic, nonsense takes the form of contradiction, the breaking of the rules of the game. This game is a purely intellectual and abstract one, and it can make no valid pronouncement about sense and nonsense outside its own field. Experience, in so far as it can be reduced to abstractions, can be handled by logic, and if the relationships run according to rule, that will make sense for the purposes of logic, and the contrary will be nonsense. By far the greater part of experience, however, is for logic neither sense nor nonsense; it is merely unmanageable, because it cannot be rendered sufficiently abstract. Next comes the scientist. His world is not wholly abstract, since his system of mental relations is meant to apply to experience. Sense from the scientific point of view will consist of those happenings and statements which conform to the particular network of mental relations, an increasingly mathematical one, which science has thus far mapped out as the pattern of the external world. All statements are required to conform to this set of relations, adopted by science as the standard of sense. The third case mentioned, the modern philosopher of language, also involves a standard set of relations, conformity with which is equivalent to sense. We find one of them, A. J. Ayer, saying (*Language, Truth and Logic*, Ch. I, p. 45), 'The utterances of the metaphysician who is attempting to expound a vision are literally senseless.' Once again the sense-and-nonsense touchstone is a pattern held in a particular mind, in this case a set of linguistic relations.

The ordinary individual, who is neither scientist, logician nor philosopher, has nevertheless a clear working knowledge of what constitutes sense and nonsense. The latter will probably take one of two forms. First, it may be a collection of words which in their internal composition of letters and syllables or in their selection and sequence do not conform to the conventional patterns of language to which the particular mind is accustomed. One's own mother-tongue is sense, the remainder are so much Greek or double dutch. Or Nonsense may appear as a collection of events or a verbal description of such a collection, where the order and relationships differ from those held to be normal. Even though the ordinary mind may not be familiar with logic or higher thought in general, it uses exactly the same standard of reference, a fixed pattern of mental relations between letters, words or events.

We can begin, therefore, by describing nonsense as a collection of words or events which in their arrangement do not fit into some recognized system in a particular mind. In practice the term 'nonsense' is more often applied to collections of words than to collections of things; this is understandable, since language is one of the mind's principal instruments for making sense of things and events. The inference is that sense no less than nonsense is largely a verbal matter, but we cannot do more than remark on this now. The appearance of nonsense—a lack of conformity in the material in question—may be due either to an absence of internal relations in the material or to the presence of a system of which the mind is unaware. (From this follows the notion of 'Chance'.) These two possibilities may look as if they amount to much the same thing, since, for the conscious mind, a relationship system which is unperceived is equivalent to there being no system at all. There is a difference, however, and one that has practical results. If you assume an absence of relations, you can get no further; but if you are ready to postulate relations as yet unperceived in the particular material, something may happen.

Our material here, self-styled Nonsense, consists in the first place of the work of Edward Lear and Lewis Carroll. Lear's Nonsense runs to some two hundred limericks, twenty nonsense songs (longer and usually narrative in character, comprising some of his best-known works such as *The Owl and the Pussy-Cat* and *The Yonghy-Bonghy-Bò*), two small collections of nonsense cookery and nonsense botany, six nonsense alphabets and two short tales in prose, *The Story of the Four Little Children Who Went Round the World*, and *The History of the Seven Families of the Lake Pipple Popple*.   Carroll's Nonsense consists of *Alice's Adventures in Wonderland, Through the Looking-Glass, The Hunting of the Snark*, and two partial Nonsense creations, *Sylvie and Bruno* and *Sylvie and Bruno Concluded*. The other works of Lear and Carroll will be available for consultation, but do not form part of the material proper.

From now on, Nonsense for us will mean primarily the work of these two, acknowledged masters of their craft, who practised Nonsense deliberately, chiefly in words, and proffered it to the ordinary mind. That mind can receive it in one of three ways. If the mind is of the extreme type of dogmatic realist, it can dismiss Nonsense as skimble-skamble stuff along with dreams, magic, poetry, religion and other such sets of mental relations which do not correspond with what this mind calls 'reality', a set of postulated relations assumed to be absolute, deviation from which can neither be tolerated nor enjoyed. A second possible attitude is to regard Nonsense as an annihilation of relations, either of language or experience, and to enjoy it as a delectable and infinite anarchy knowing no rules, liberating the mind from any form of order or system. The third possibility is to regard Nonsense as a structure held together by valid mental relations.

With the first of these three there is no arguing. Lear, Carroll, this book, and much else besides, are not for them. The argument here lies between the second and third. Many people, I believe, would hold the second view: that Nonsense is just what is *not sense*, and any attempt at systematization could only injure its subtle and insubstantial pleasure. One meets the same argument in regard to poetry: that its essence is of such a kind that to bring intellectual scrutiny to bear upon it is at best mistaken pedantry and at worst sacrilege. This is not, however, how poets think about poetry, nor, perhaps, Nonsense-writers about Nonsense. It makes Nonsense a product of chance operating at the mental level, comparable with Surrealist

literature which seeks to suppress any conscious control of
the mind's flow of images.

There are a number of things to be said against this.
First, Nonsense as practised by Lear and Carroll does not,
even on a slight acquaintance, give the impression of being
something without laws and subject to chance, or something without limits, tending towards infinity. Sir Edmund
Strachey, writing about Lear's Nonsense in the *Quarterly
Review*, 1888, called it a child of genius, one of the Fine
Arts. Now a Fine Art is not the product of chance, nor is
it the result of absence of limitation, for the mind can do
nothing with infinity, that most unmanageable commodity.
The unfailing mental delight, if one may use such a
phrase, afforded by Lear and Carroll does not suggest
an endless succession of random events, than which nothing
is more boring, nor does it point to a universe out of control, frighteningly akin to lunacy. The mention of Art in
connection with this Nonsense and the absence of bore-
dom or disquiet suggest that we may be able to rule out
both chance and surrealism. We are going to assume that
Nonsense is not merely the denial of sense, a random rever-
sal of ordinary experience and an escape from the limitations of everyday life into a haphazard infinity, but is on
the contrary a carefully limited world, controlled and
directed by reason, a construction subject to its own laws.

The argument that this will destroy the very inwardness
of Nonsense is surely mistaken. If a mental structure of
whatever kind cannot submit to examination then there is
something shaky and insecure about it, and this is as true
of Nonsense as of anything else. Poetry, for instance,
does not collapse at the touch of logic, and there is no
reason why Nonsense should do so either. To fear a logical
approach is in some way to impugn the integrity of the
subject matter. There is something bogus about these
mystical essences which are said to evaporate on close in-
spection. Nonsense, with its immense sense of balance and
safety, is better built than that; one might as well expect the

splendid vision of a great building to disappear in smoke because the mind happened to know its proportions in terms of mathematics. There is on record at least one example of a vision being submitted to exact measurement with a yardstick, and neither the angel nor the prophet Ezekiel seems to have been troubled by a sense of futile desecration.

If Nonsense is an art, it must have its own laws of construction, and the investigation of these brings us at once into touch with logic, as a study of mental relations within a particular field. The limitation of the field will explain certain omissions. For instance, this is not going to be a study of Humour or of the Comic. Laughter is incidental to Nonsense but not essential to it. Many people confuse the two, but a moment's recollection of the work of Lear or Carroll shows that much that happens in the world of Nonsense is not comic at all. Neither shall we be concerned with psychoanalysis. This would be a possible approach to the minds of both writers, but the aim here is logical and not psychological. Psychology is concerned with the interpretation, according to some particular theory, of the products of the imagination in terms of individual experience. For the logician, however, even for so amateur a one as myself, this question of interpretation does not arise, and the imaginary world may be considered as a valid structure with its own consistency which does not need translation into the terms of some other system or way of thinking. This will not be an attempt to find out what the Old Man with a Beard or the Mock Turtle stand for—it suffices that they stand. We shall not bring to light the 'Sub-conscious' of either artist, a term I do not propose to employ at all. What we can hope to do is to discover the structure of Nonsense itself, and to do this there will be no need to embrace any particular school of thought, for logic has this great advantage over psychology, that the mind's processes in logic are not a matter of controversy. And after all, one of our two Nonsense writers was a professional logician himself.

Chapter 2

A DOUBLE RULE OF THREE

I T S E E M S awkward at first to have to think about Lear and Carroll together. The world of the Alices and that of the limericks seem so very different. Lear's Nonsense is simple, concrete, descriptive and unconversational for the most part, with far more verse than prose. Carroll's Nonsense takes the form of consecutive narrative, with much more prose than verse, essentially conversational (for when Alice has no one to talk to she talks to herself), and at times highly abstract and complex in its language. The two seem to be completely different, with only the name of Nonsense to hold them together. It looks as if it might have been simpler to deal with each of these highly individual writers separately rather than both at once.

This is in fact what has been done in the past. A good deal has been written about Carroll, mainly biographical or panegyrical in character. Lear has been less worked over. Apart from Mr. Angus Davidson's comparatively recent biography of him,[1] and the role he plays in M. Emile Cammaerts' *The Poetry of Nonsense*, he has not attracted study. This is understandable, for Carroll's more elaborately articulated Nonsense offers better material for analysis. M. Cammaerts' book is the only full-length work known to me which studies both writers.

Our aim is not to discover anything new about these two men as individuals, nor to explain them and their respective brands of Nonsense one at a time. It is to construct something, to build up a way of thinking about Nonsense. If we are working on the right lines, we may discover a structure common to the works of both men.

[1] *Edward Lear: Landscape Painter and Nonsense Poet*, John Murray, London, 1938.

B

We shall only find it, however, by building a structure ourselves. Compared with the more accepted forms of literary criticism, this is rather as if, instead of playing patience on a flat green table with the cards neatly arranged in numbers and suits, we insist on building card houses. The finished product will be delicate in its balance and easy to demolish; but by that very quality it may fit a world of Wonderland which in its turn was said to be 'nothing but a pack of cards,' and which in the end fell in confusion about feminine ears.

Despite the difficulty of having two things to think about, there are two advantages to it as well. The first is that relations of comparison can be introduced, likeness and unlikeness, very useful relations to build with, and obviously unusable where the subject-matter is single, since a thing cannot be either like or unlike itself. The second lies in the fact that one of these worlds seems simple and the other complex; for we can perhaps hope to apply to each the methods of the other, to discover complexity beneath the apparent simplicity of Lear, and a simplicity beneath Carroll's complication.

Relations of comparison have already been employed, in noticing certain dissimilarities between these two worlds. It may be useful now, not to leave too one-sided an impression, to see some of the resemblances, not only between the two worlds of Nonsense but also between the men who created them. To take the authors first, they were, of course, fellow-Englishmen, and near-contemporaries. Lear's first *Book of Nonsense* appeared in 1846, *Alice's Adventures in Wonderland* in 1865, though it had been composed three years earlier. Neither man married. Each was an extreme stickler for precision in daily life; this is well known as regards Carroll, whose life and manners are in any case more familiar than those of Lear, but it is interesting that the latter also had this characteristic to a marked degree. His biographer comments on the meticulous recording of detail in Lear's journal—hotel bills,

prices of tickets, times of trains, names of stopping-places—
and adds, 'Every action is timed, not only by the day but
by the hour' (Davidson, Ch. XV, p. 229). Both men were
afraid of dogs. Both maintained an enormous correspondence. Both had religious convictions, with a great mistrust
of Catholicism. This is a jumbled list of likenesses, but not
an unsuggestive one.

A similar crop of small points of resemblance can be
gathered from the Nonsense. We need not consider the
possibility of mutual plagiarism; there is no evidence that
either man was familiar with the other's work, and much
speculation by critics has taken the question no further.
The likenesses do not in any case suggest borrowings which
would have been pointless; rather, a curious rapprochement now and again between the forms of Nonsense.[1]

(1) He was black in the face, and they scarcely could trace
    The least likeness to what he had been:
    While so great was his fright that his waistcoat turned
      white—
    A wonderful thing to be seen!
                    (CARROLL, Fit the Seventh, H.S.)

There was an old man of Port Grigor,
Whose actions were noted for vigour;
He stood on his head, till his waistcoat turned red,
That eclectic old man of Port Grigor.
                         (LEAR, M.N.)

(2)   The Dormouse again took a minute to think about it,
and then said 'It was a treacle-well.'
                (*A Mad Tea Party*, A.A.W.)

    They found nothing at all except some wide and deep
pits full of Mulberry Jam.
             (*The Four Little Children*, N.S.B.)

(3) Put cats in the coffee and mice in the tea—
    And welcome Queen Alice with thirty-times-three!
                (*Queen Alice*, T.L.G.)

[1] I have used the following editions: *The Complete Works of Lewis
Carroll*, Nonesuch Press, London, 1939; and *The Complete Nonsense
of Edward Lear*, Faber & Faber, London 1947.

There was an Old Person of Ewell,
Who chiefly subsisted on gruel;
But to make it more nice, he inserted some mice,
Which refreshed that Old Person of Ewell.

(B.N.)

Another rather similar mixture may be seen in the following pair of examples:—

And the banquet, so plainly provided,
Shall round into rosebuds and rice.

(*To the Rescue!*, S.B.C.)

And she made him a feast at his earnest wish
Of eggs and buttercups fried with fish.

(*The Pobble Who Has No Toes*, L.L.)

Each writer invents a living creature combined with a
corkscrew. Carroll's creation is the tove in *Jabberwocky*,
described by Humpty Dumpty as 'something like badgers
—they're something like lizards—and they're something
like corkscrews'. Lear's is a bird, 'the Fimble Fowl, with
a corkscrew leg' which appears in *The Quangle Wangle's
Hat*. Each has an animal that cannot jump and wants to
learn the art from one which can:—

There was a Frog that wandered by . . .
And said 'O Pig, what makes you cry?'
And bitter was that Pig's reply,
   'Because I cannot jump!'

(*The Pig-Tale*, S.B.C.)

'My life is a bore in this nasty pond,
And I long to go out in the world beyond!
I wish I could hop like you!'
Said the Duck to the Kangaroo.

(*The Duck and the Kangaroo*, N.S.B.)

Each magnifies the size of dogs, even small ones, in proportion to human beings. In Carroll this takes the form of
Alice's encounter with the puppy in Wonderland: 'An
enormous puppy was looking down at her with large
round eyes . . . she was terribly frightened all the time at
the thought that it might be hungry, in which case it

would be very likely to eat her up in spite of all her coaxing.' In Lear's Nonsense the victim *is* eaten:—

> There was an Old Man of Leghorn,
> The smallest as ever was born;
> But quickly snapped up he, was once by a puppy,
> Who devoured that Old Man of Leghorn.
>
> (B.N.)

In the illustrations to this and the other limerick which begins 'There was an Old Man of Ancona, Who found a small dog with no owner' (M.N.), the dog is depicted as much larger than the human being.

Each writer introduces an owl in company with a feline. Lear's Owl and Pussy-Cat is perhaps his best-known work, but there is a similar pair in Carroll:—

> I passed by his garden, and marked, with one eye,
> How the Owl and the Panther were sharing a pie.
>
> (*The Lobster-Quadrille*, A.A.W.)

This in turn has another echo in Lear, who also produces a bird with a pie, though a parrot and not an owl, in one of the Nonsense alphabets: 'The Perpendicular Purple Polly, who read the Newspaper and ate Parsnip Pie with his spectacles' (M.N.). Each has someone hidden in an umbrella. Carroll says that Tweedledee, after Tweedledum had discovered the broken rattle, 'immediately sat down on the ground, and tried to hide himself under the umbrella'. Lear's figure comes from the same Nonsense alphabet as the polly, 'The Umbrageous Umbrella-maker, whose face nobody ever saw, because it was always covered by his Umbrella.' There are double examples of creatures involved, quite literally, with worsted:—

> The kitten had been having a grand game of romps with the ball of worsted Alice had been trying to wind up, and had been rolling it up and down till it had all come undone again.
>
> (*Looking-Glass House*, T.L.G.)

> They perceived an unusual and gratifying spectacle, namely, a large number of Crabs and Crawfish—perhaps

six or seven hundred—sitting by the water-side, and en-
deavouring to disentangle a vast heap of pale pink worsted.
(*The Four Little Children*, N.S.B.)

There are even odd verbal approximations, as in this
pair:—

Little Birds are hiding
Crimes in carpet-bags.
(*The Pig-Tale*, S.B.C.)

The Goodnatured Grey Gull, who carried the Old Owl,
and his Crimson Carpet-bag, across the river, because
he could not swim.

(M.N.)

There is no reason yet to lend undue importance to
these small resemblances; but at least they show how these
two worlds may throw out feelers, so to speak, towards one
another. If we can in the same way move in towards the
centre, there may be something to be discovered where the
two meet in the middle. What one needs is some form of
system or construction, already in existence and familiar
to the mind, which would be common ground for both
writers; and there is one literary genre, a childishly simple
one, that looks as if it would fill the bill—Nursery Rhymes.

In this connection, as in so many others, Lear seems to
differ from Carroll, for he makes no direct use of Nursery
Rhymes at all. No characters from them are embodied in
his Nonsense, nor does he either use or parody the rhymes
themselves. In view of this it seems strange to suggest that
they may form a bridge between his work and Carroll's;
but the fact that they are not explicitly in his work does
not mean that they are foreign to it. The more one reads
him, the more echoes of Nursery Rhymes one comes
across. M. Cammaerts in *The Poetry of Nonsense*, p. 2, says
of Lear that the idea of writing geographical limericks
was suggested to him by a friend who drew his attention
to the nursery rhyme, 'There was an old man of Tobago',
and adds, 'The connection between modern and old non-

sense poetry is thus significantly established. It is to the
nursery rhyme that we owe the nonsense songs.' I would
sooner say that the Nursery Rhymes and Lear's verses
have affinities, and leave it at that; but the affinities are
certainly there. Lear's Old Man of the Isles who 'sung
high dum diddle, and played on the fiddle' recalls *Hey
diddle diddle*.[1] There is a shadow of the Nursery Rhyme,

> Hannah Bantry
> In the pantry
> Eating a mutton bone. . . .

in Lear's verse:—

> There was a young person of Bantry
> Who frequently slept in the pantry.

The 'pig' and 'wig' rhyme which appears in such jingles as

> As I was going to Bonner
> I met a pig
> Without a wig
> Upon my word and honour.
>
> Barber, barber, shave a pig.
> How many hairs to make a wig?

has a good run in Lear's limericks also:—

> There was an old man of Messina
> Whose daughter was named Opsibeena;
> She wore a small wig, and rode out on a pig,
> To the perfect delight of Messina.
>
> (M.N.)
>
> There was an Old Person of Cheadle,
> Who was put in the stocks by the beadle;
> For stealing some pigs, some coats and some wigs,
> That horrible Person of Cheadle.

The old person of Grange who 'sailed to St. Blubb in a
waterproof tub' reminds one of the Three Men of Gotham,

---

[1] Most of the Nursery Rhymes in this book are given from memory.
I have used as a work of reference *The Nursery Rhymes of England*
edited by James Halliwell, 1842, but where this differed from the
versions I knew I have preferred the living tradition to the printed
word.

who went to sea in a bowl; the Jumblies go one better
and go to sea in a sieve. Miss Muffet shadows the Old
Person of Bromley who 'sate in the dust, eating spiders
and crust', just as Willie Winkie lurks behind this verse
in Lear's self-portrait,

> When he walks in a waterproof white,
> The children run after him so!
> Calling out, 'He's come out in his night—
> Gown, that crazy old Englishman, oh!'

Judging by these examples, Lear seems to construct a
world that is like that of Nursery Rhyme, but does not
comment on the fact.

With Carroll things are different. His world is in many
ways less akin to the Nursery Rhyme world, yet it is he
who introduces these rhymes and their characters directly
into his Nonsense. In *Alice in Wonderland* there is only one
example, the rhyme about the Queen of Hearts, which
Alice herself quotes; but the characters from this one
rhyme people nearly half the book. In *Through the Looking-
Glass* Nursery Rhymes are more plentiful: Tweedledum
and Tweedledee, Humpty Dumpty, the Lion and the
Unicorn, the parody of *Rockabye baby on the tree-top* which
begins, 'Hush-a-by lady, in Alice's lap!' and a mention of
'Here we go round the mulberry bush'. 'How many miles
to Babylon?' is quoted in *Sylvie and Bruno*. The most concentrated example of the introduction of Nursery Rhymes
comes in the chapter *To the Rescue!* in *Sylvie and Bruno
Concluded*. It is a parody of Swinburne's *By the North Sea*
which begins thus,

> A land that is lonelier than ruin,
> A sea that is stranger than death:
> Far fields that a rose never blew in,
> Wan waste where the winds lack breath

and so on, in a characteristic but not the best Swinburnian
manner. Carroll turns it into a version of 'There was a
little man and he had a little gun'. It is too long to give in

full, unfortunately, for it is most enjoyable; but these are
the three middle verses:—

> He has loaded with bullet and powder:
>   His footfall is noiseless as air:
> But the Voices grow louder and louder,
>   And bellow, and bluster, and blare.
> They bristle before him and after,
>   They flutter above and below,
> Shrill shriekings of lubberly laughter,
>   Weird wailings of woe!
>
> They echo without him, within him:
>   They thrill through his whiskers and beard:
> Like a teetotum seeming to spin him,
>   With sneers never hitherto sneered.
> 'Avengement,' they cry, 'on our Foelet!
>   Let the Manikin weep for our wrongs!
> Let us drench him, from toplet to toelet,
>   With Nursery Songs!
>
> 'He shall muse upon "Hey! Diddle! Diddle!"
>   On the Cow that surmounted the Moon:
> He shall rave of the Cat and the Fiddle,
>   And the Dish that eloped with the Spoon:
> And his soul shall be sad for the Spider
>   When Miss Muffet was sipping her whey,
> That so tenderly sat down beside her
>   And scared her away!'

I think we are justified in regarding Nursery Rhymes as
a useful addition to the Nonsense structure we are studying, and it is interesting that they, like the more literary
forms of Nonsense, have flourished more in England than
anywhere else. The political nature of some of them might
seem to set them in a different class from the works of
Lear and Carroll, though the latter has been credited
with satiric intentions by certain critics. Their historical
origins are unimportant here, however, compared with
the fact of their incorporation into popular tradition and
their survival as Nonsense constructions long after their
contemporary implications are forgotten. As constructions

of this kind, they give rise to problems of their own. Are they, for instance, an embryonic form of poetry, containing the germs of full development into poetry but inhibited in some way, so that they have never grown up? Or are they an alternative development, full-grown according to their own laws but differing by those laws themselves from poetry proper? This question looks as if it might apply to Nonsense as a whole, but it must wait for the present. It may seem as if we have merely complicated the field of enquiry by adding this third element, that of Nursery Rhyme, to it; but we have seen already that we might have to simplify and to complicate our subject-matter. The only trouble is that, Nonsense-fashion, we shall probably have to proceed in both directions at once. Here, looking for unity, we have turned two into three. It is rather like Carroll's verse,

> He thought he saw a Garden Door
> That opened with a Key:
> He looked again and found it was
> A Double Rule of Three.

A Double Rule of Three has an advantage, however; it is an abstract and can be worked inside the head, as garden doors cannot.

Chapter 3

THE RIGHT WORDS

S O F A R we have been talking about the 'world' of Nonsense. That is one way of thinking about it, but we must be careful not to imagine that this world of Nonsense is a world of things. Perhaps this sounds foolishly obvious, but the distinction between things and notions of things is not always an easy one for the mind to maintain; and it is all the harder when, as in Nonsense, the language is simple and the subject-matter concrete, causing the mind to pass rapidly through the words, so to speak, to the things to which they refer. When Lear remarks, 'There was an old man in a barge, Whose nose was exceedingly large', the mind on meeting that says to itself, 'Now here are three things, a man, a barge and a big nose.' The same happens when Carroll says, 'The March Hare had just upset the milk jug into his plate.'

This holds good whether the thing referred to actually exists or not. With either a lion *or* a unicorn the mind will say, 'Here are things for me to play with'; and it will be wrong, at least in this world of Nonsense which is not a universe of things but of words and ways of using them, plus a certain amount of pictorial illustration. Once this is grasped, the investigation can begin on the right lines. We shall know that we are not dealing with cows sitting in red morocco armchairs making toast at the parlour fire (M.N.), or with chessmen sliding down the poker into an ashy grate (T.L.G.). We are dealing with words. In Nonsense all the world is paper and all the seas are ink. This may seem cramping, but it has one great advantage: one need not discuss the so-called unreality or reality of the Nonsense world. The scope of enquiry is limited to what goes on inside a mind. No matter how often Lear may put before us such phrases as 'The Broom and the Shovel, the Poker and Tongs', or Carroll begin a tale, in the grammar he considered appropriate to Bruno, 'Once there were a Pig, and a Accordion, and two jars of Orange-Marmalade', we do not have shovels and pigs and jamjars inside our heads. Only the words will be there, and they are enough to start with.

Now it is an interesting fact that whereas Lear uses words simply as a means of communication with another mind, apart from Nonsense words which will be considered later, Carroll, though his language is no less lucid, seems to spend much of his time watching the language process itself. He is almost as much interested in the system as in the substance. His works are not merely in words, they are very frequently about words. The Alices show this particularly clearly. In his Nonsense world Carroll endows practically everything with the power of speech, so that endless exchanges of words become possible. Lear, in eight of his longer songs and in his two prose tales, also permits animals and objects to speak, but he does not carry the process nearly so far. In the Alices, flowers, insects, animals, legs of mutton, Christmas puddings, playing cards and chessmen, can all speak, and the result is that they and Alice are perpetually involved in a particular kind of dialectic. ' "It's really dreadful," she muttered to herself, "the way all the creatures argue. It's enough to drive one crazy!" ' That is in Wonderland, and there, too, occurs Alice's complaint, after she has tried to recite *How doth the little* . . . , that 'those are not the right words'; in the same way, after the recitation of *You are old, Father William* at the Caterpillar's request, she says 'some of the words have got altered'. Throughout both books there are constant demands for verbal precision, such as the March Hare's remark, 'Then you should say what you mean,' or this passage from *Queen Alice:*—

'I only said "if"!' poor Alice pleaded in a piteous tone. The two Queens looked at each other, and the Red

Queen remarked, with a little shudder, 'She *says* she only said "if"——'

'But she said a great deal more than that!' the White Queen moaned, wringing her hands. 'Oh, ever so much more than that!'

'So you did, you know,' the Red Queen said to Alice. 'Always speak the truth—think before you speak—and write it down afterwards.'

In Looking-Glass country there is a wood where things have no names. There is a possibility of using another tongue—'Speak in French when you ca'n't think of the English for a thing. The conversation between Alice and Humpty Dumpty is about little else but words, and at the end of the book, language, in the form of an introduction ('It isn't etiquette to cut anyone you've been introduced to. Remove the joint!'), comes between Alice and her food, just as at the beginning of Wonderland she finds a jar with words on it—ORANGE MARMALADE—but nothing inside. In *The Hunting of the Snark* the theme is still there, though with a good deal less emphasis. Echoes of the Alices occur:—

> The loss of his clothes hardly mattered, because
> He had seven coats on when he came,
> With three pairs of boots—but the worst of it was
> He had wholly forgotten his name.
>
> .   .   .   .   .   .
>
> 'I said it in Hebrew—I said it in Dutch—
> I said it in German and Greek—
> But I wholly forgot (and it vexes me much)
> That English is what you speak!'

In Fit the Sixth there is a parallel of the Court Scene in Wonderland, a trial being the perfect setting, naturally, for verbal dialectic. In the two parts of *Sylvie and Bruno* the interest in language has practically died out, apart from Bruno's annoying verbal quibbles, such as:—

> 'I wonder you've the face to tell me such fibs!' cried the Gardener.
>
> To which Bruno wisely replied, 'Oo don't want a *face* to tell fibs wiz—only a *mouf*!'

This type of thing, with the attempt to reproduce Bruno's baby talk and an occasional pun, is all that is left. It is interesting that the usual evaluation of this Nonsense, with the Alices at the top, the Snark rather lower and *Sylvie and Bruno* lower again, should coincide with the breadth and virtuosity with which the language theme is developed.

It is Carroll, too, who makes use of pun and parody; there are only very occasional puns in Lear's work ('The Geese, having webs to their feet, caught quantities of flies, which they ate for dinner'—*The Seven Families*, N.S.B.) and no parody at all. When Carroll needs incarnations of lunacy, he takes them from two current verbal expressions, 'mad as a hatter' and 'mad as a March hare'. His Looking-Glass insects grow out of words, and from a dragonfly is created a snapdragon fly. The difference between the methods of Carroll and Lear can be seen in the difference between this creation of the former and the Plum-pudding Flea of the latter, from *The Seven Families*, the one being the extension of a chance of language, the other a direct product of the imagination.

This is the first hint of something important: that in the Alices themselves may be found the principles on which Nonsense is constructed. Lear provides Nonsense in an almost perfect state of simplicity, where the principles are acted on but not stated. With Carroll things seem to be different, for though he too is constructing Nonsense in words he is at the same time thinking and writing about words, and this may provide clues, even if, since this is Nonsense, the clues may seem a little odd.

The Nonsense of Lear and of Nursery Rhyme is almost entirely in verse; that of Carroll is in verse and prose, but there is much more of the latter than the former. It may be that Nonsense goes better in verse than in prose. If so, we might expect to find Carroll's pure Nonsense in his verse, while the prose will provide the commentary. In this case Carroll's verse will probably have closer affinities with the

Nursery Rhyme and the work of Lear, which are also related each to each. In the greater complexity of Carroll's prose, however, lies the hope of elucidating the problem, for it may show us things that would lie hidden for ever in the tight and perfect little systems of Nonsense verse pure and simple. It is interesting that every time a set of verses appears in the Alices it becomes a subject for discussion and argument. The discussion may be brief, as in the case of 'Twinkle, twinkle'; but more often it is protracted, as with both verses of ''Tis the voice of the lobster', the verses beginning 'They told me you had been to her' which are read at the Knave of Hearts' trial, and, most protracted of all, *Jabberwocky*. There is no reason why this should be so. It is one of the many features of the Alices which one unthinkingly accepts; but it is rather strange. Most writers who introduce songs or poems into their stories do not set their characters arguing about them. If, however, this suggestion is somewhere near the mark, and the verses in the Alices are the Nonsense practice while the prose at the same time gives some of the theory, the arguments take on a new significance.

We need to be clear about the nature of the guidebook we have got. In one sense it is less a guidebook than a set of clues in a treasure hunt, for the directions are anything but straightforward. A book that is a guide to itself sounds distinctly nonsensical, but in fact that principle holds good for any system. A system can only exhibit or demonstrate itself, and that is as true of Nonsense as it is of pure poetry, for instance. Mr. De La Mare puts these two, Nonsense and pure poetry, side by side in his work on Carroll,[1] and that is interesting, for they are near contemporaries, and it is possible that Carroll is the English manifestation of the French logic and rigour which produced the work of Mallarmé, also labelled nonsense in its time. Carroll is perhaps the equivalent of that attempt to render language a closed and consistent system on its own; but he made his

[1] *Lewis Carroll*, p. 16.

35/46

experiment not upon poetry but upon Nonsense. Where the Frenchman's poems may be taken to be a commentary upon poetry itself, the Englishman makes his Nonsense a commentary upon Nonsense, no less obscure or rigorous in its nature, and sharing that tendency towards logic and mathematics in which he had the advantage of his French counterpart, since he was a professional.

Such a commentary will not give directions, nor will it describe its own nature in so many words. What is to be conveyed will have to be gathered not from *what* is said so much as *how* it is said, as if the content lay hidden in the structure of the work. Where this unity exists between form and content, the 'meaning', if such it may be called, will be difficult of access, since it will reside in the structure, and that has first to be apprehended, as in a mathematical or logical problem. Only then will the work give up its secrets, and that is true of the Alices as well. It may seem strange to suggest that the Alices are obscure, when they are always supposed to be of a limpid clarity. The point is that though their vocabulary is simple, a characteristic they share with pure poetry in general, their structure is not, and it is this alone which can tell us what the work is about, for it is a work about itself. There is one comforting thing, however, about this kind of investigation: the odds are that one structure will resemble another and there will be possibilities of comparison. In the last analysis, structures are the only things which the mind can prove to be alike. Presumably a structure totally unlike any other would be unknowable.

Nonsense can take the form either of prose or verse, and so one might think that either prose or poetry, two familiar structures of language, might help by way of analogy. In fact, however, they do not. Prose cannot serve as a yardstick because for one thing Nonsense much prefers to be in verse, and for another the ordinary purpose of prose is to make sense, while Nonsense proclaims by its very name that its nature is to do the opposite. Poetry, however, is no help either. Nonsense may take the form of verse, but we should presumably agree that there is a distinction between this and poetry. This distinction may lie in what one might call the dream element in poetry, its ambiguity, its imagery by which, as in a dream, fusions may take place between images in the mind, its sudden breaks in sequence. Poetry, so Coleridge said, is at its best when only imperfectly understood. There is nothing of this in Nonsense verse. Far from being ambiguous, shifting and dreamlike, it is concrete, clear and wholly comprehensible:—

> 'You have baked me too brown, I must sugar my hair'.
> (*The Lobster-Quadrille*, A.A.W.)

> A sea-green Porpoise carried away
>   His wrapper of scarlet flannel.
> (*The Pobble Who Has No Toes*, L.L.)

> The Queen was in the parlour,
>   Eating bread and honey.

Ambiguous? Only imperfectly understood? They are as clear as day.

Nonsense verse is too precise to be akin to poetry. It seems much nearer logic than dream. Critics have denied this, M. Cammaerts for example, who says, 'Nonsense poems and stories . . . do not tell a connected story; indeed their main purpose is to upset all logic, for they scorn any rational or comprehensible language' (*The Poetry of Nonsense*, p. 15). Experience does not bear this out. Poets may, by the nature of their art, have dealings with fine frenzy, madness and dream, but the Nonsense writer may not. Nonsense is very careful about the point. Carroll introduces a hint of lunacy into Wonderland with the Mad Hatter and March Hare, but this episode is prepared for by the Cheshire Cat's remarks:—

> 'But I don't want to go among mad people,' Alice remarked.
> 'Oh, you ca'n't help that,' said the Cat: 'we're all mad here. I'm mad. You're mad.'
> 'How do you know I'm mad?' said Alice.

C

'You must be,' said the Cat, 'or you wouldn't have come here.'

(*Pig and Pepper*, A.A.W.)

At the end of *Through the Looking-Glass* where the vision starts getting out of control and threatens to turn into madness or nightmare, Alice puts an abrupt end to it, saying, 'I ca'n't stand this any longer!' and waking herself up. There is one case of sudden madness in Carroll, in *The Hunting of the Snark:*—

> To the horror of all who were present that day,
>   He uprose in full evening dress,
> And with senseless grimaces endeavoured to say
>   What his tongue could no longer express.
>
> Down he sank in a chair—ran his hands through his hair—
>   And chanted in mimsiest tones
> Words whose utter inanity proved his insanity,
>   While he rattled a couple of bones.

This example jars as something unpleasant and in poor taste. Lear avoids dream and madness altogether. His one character who had tendencies in that direction is dealt with firmly:—

> There was an Old Person of Rheims,
> Who was troubled with horrible dreams;
> So, to keep him awake, they fed him on cake,
> Which amused that Old Person of Rheims.

(B.N.)

If neither prose nor poetry can provide the necessary structure for Nonsense, is there some other system by which language could be organized into an independent and consistent, if nonsensical, structure? The answer, or hint after hint at a possible answer, shouts at us from the Alices; and yet here again we have grown so used to these stories that their peculiar features are blurred in our minds and we miss the point. In Wonderland Alice observes the Fish Footman delivering to the Frog Footman 'an invitation from the Queen to play croquet'. When she eventually reaches the rose garden she finds it tenanted by playing cards, and she herself a little later joins in the croquet game. Looking-Glass begins with a diagram of a problem in chess. The principal characters are chess pieces, and the landscape that Alice sees from the hill in Looking-Glass country is a chequerboard:—

> 'I declare it's marked out just like a large chess-board!' Alice said at last. 'There ought to be some men moving about somewhere—and so there are!' she added in a tone of delight, and her heart began to beat quick with excitement as she went on. 'It's a great huge game of chess that's being played—all over the world—if this *is* the world at all, you know!'
>
> (The Garden of Live Flowers)

Remarks of the following kind seem to say the same thing:—

> 'I love my love with an H,' Alice couldn't help beginning, 'because he is Happy. I hate him with an H, because he is Hideous. I fed him with—with—Ham-sandwiches and Hay. His name is Haigha, and he lives——'
>
> 'He lives on the Hill,' the King remarked simply, without the least idea that he was joining in the game.
>
> (The Lion and the Unicorn, T.L.G.)
>
> 'In that case we start afresh,' said Humpty Dumpty, 'and it's my turn to choose a subject——' ('He talks about it just as if it was a game!' thought Alice.)
>
> (Humpty Dumpty, T.L.G.)

'Just as if it was a game'—suppose it is a game. Could Nonsense be an attempt at reorganizing language, not according to the rules of prose or poetry in the first place but according to those of Play? I do not mean here the simplest forms of games of energy and horseplay, but the more highly developed and complicated types of play. Each game of this type is an enclosed whole, with its own rigid laws which cannot be questioned within the game itself; if you put yourself inside the system which is the game, you bind yourself by that system's laws, and so incidentally attain that particular sense of freedom which games have to offer. A game may presumably be regarded as an independent system with its own brand of relationship structure. Chance may enter into it, but it is not necessarily an essential element. The International Chess Code defines Chess as 'a game in the play of which there is no element of chance'. A game is, if considered in the abstract, a system in the mind, requiring at least one mind for the playing of it, requiring also, and this is important, a set of objects, or one single object, with which it is to be played. It appeals to an undying instinct in human beings of all ages, gives delight while limiting emotion to that generated by the game itself, resists intrusion and affords the mind a clearly defined field in which to carry on the activity proper to the game in hand.

Since Nonsense is made up of language, its playthings will be words. These are not simple objects like tennis balls or tiddlywink counters; strictly speaking, they are scarcely objects at all. The nature of words, half abstract and half concrete, will affect the types and variations of play, just as the fact that it is being played with will affect the language in its turn. The notion of a Game, however, may give us the analogy of structure we have been looking for. This is not going to lead to frivolity and emptiness. St. Thomas Aquinas compares wisdom and games by saying that each is to be pursued for its own sake. The *play* of thought is a normal enough phrase. A mental structure need be no less excellent in its design just because it is a game. Any structure is worth studying, an exercise in mapping relations and tracing out a peculiar logic. With Nonsense we are faced with the finished product, and we have to discover the field of the game and the rules by which it is played. It is worth noticing that so far we have collected, by way of assistance, logic, dialectic and St. Thomas Aquinas. Things begin to look mediæval, and promising.

Chapter 4

WORD PLAY AND DIALECTIC

W<small>E HAD</small> better hazard a definition of a Game at this point, and work onwards from there:—

A GAME: the active manipulation, serving no useful purpose, of a certain object or class of objects, concrete or mental, within a limited field of space and time and according to fixed rules, with the aim of producing a given result despite the opposition of chance and/or opponents.

This will not fit very loosely organized games of make-believe, but it will cover games of such widely different types as chess, cards, football, tennis, snakes and ladders, tig, hopscotch, spillikins, crossword puzzles, rounders and tiddlywinks, and that seems good enough to start with, though almost every term in the definition will need discussion and expansion. We can begin by taking the two fundamentals of any human play situation, a mind to effect the manipulation, and something to be manipulated.

These are the essentials of play, and three things follow from them. First, the player must consent to play. Individuals can, of course, be compelled to take part in a game, but in such circumstances of constraint the game for the individual concerned ceases to be a game and becomes a task or imposition. Secondly, the player must have something to manipulate; you cannot play with the totally non-existent. Thirdly, whatever it is that is to be manipulated in play must be within your control. It looks from these pointers as if one of the aspects of play is a deliberate attempt to establish mastery over certain objects in experience, a view supported by writers on the subject, who lay emphasis on the importance of play to children as a means of enabling them to gain control over objects of experience, the movements of their own bodies, the special properties of such things as water and sand, and so on. It has become a commonplace that the best objects for a child's play are not elaborate toys but ordinary everyday objects.

The fact that play consists in establishing mastery over something limits the field in which it can be exercised. Man is small and the range of his mind is small, too, and the number of the things within his control is very limited. You cannot play with great things, as the Voice out of the Whirlwind pointed out to Job, saying of Leviathan, 'Wilt thou play with him as with a bird? or wilt thou bind him for thy maidens?' You cannot play with things whose properties are wholly or even mainly beyond your control; you cannot play catch-as-catch-can with a group of jaguars, for instance, instead of a group of children. The range of playthings is limited to those things which man can control, either inside or outside himself. I said a moment ago that the mind could only control small things; by this I mean it can only control those things which present themselves in the form of small units, capable of being looked at as a series of distinct individuals. The essential in playthings is that they should be comparatively small, and should be separate units. How much of life presents itself in this form, and what things, either inside or outside the mind, are small, stable and controllable?

Outside the mind, in the world of normal experience, the objects which fulfil these conditions are those that surround human beings in everyday life. We assume that things as we know them, with their respective properties, are constant, and individually separate from one another. Chairs do not move, we believe, unless we move them, nor do they turn into bicycles overnight, nor if they are of a yellow colour do they suddenly turn red, or prove to be of steel instead of wood; so, too, we distinguish one chair from another, a row of chairs being a row of distinct units. Our own bodies are units likewise, and they are assumed to work on the same principles, so that people do not suddently become sheep, or vanish away altogether. Thus with a solid controllable series of chairs, a series of bodies, and a sequence of sounds which can be controlled by being stopped and started at will, and the help of a series of numbers (since the total of chairs must be one less than the total of bodies) the game of Musical Chairs can be played. Like all other games it depends upon the integrity and separation of the units, each unit remaining constant in itself and separate from every other unit. Incidentally, these are not merely the conditions for a game; they are also the conditions for sense and sanity. Hallucination can very well take the form of running things together, and when this happens, activity becomes less and less possible.

Inside the mind the same thing holds good. One cannot control hallucinations, nightmares, dreams or the more violent emotions. They are not capable of being broken down into distinct units which would make them controllable, and none of them, therefore, can be played with. Only pieces of our mental furniture which appear to be capable of resolution into simple and distinct elements are suitable for play. Whatever form of activity the mind may indulge in, it has to have its material first in little bits. That is partly why language is so important to the mind, for language splits experience into small labelled units which the mind can then manipulate, and by the help of which it can mentally arrange experience.

Games in the mind have to be played with small units. Two systems of such units, language and number, are the chief sources of mental playthings and it is on these two that we shall concentrate rather than on any supposedly distinct faculties of the mind, such as memory or imagination, which are also involved in mental play. Memory, imagination, reason and so on will all come into the game, but I do not propose to discuss them separately. The reason for this is partly that the thinking mind (which is also the playing mind) works with units no matter what gear it is in, so to speak. Partly, too, I am compelled to concentrate on the mind's units and what I am tempted to call its Unitary Method because I am in a sense playing a game myself in the writing of this, and I cannot play with the notions of memory and reason and so on, since they cannot be split up or controlled. Number and language, or to put it a little differently, numbers and words, make better playthings.

Numbers 1, 2, 3, 4 and so on make ideal play material for the mind, for each number is a unit, capable of being broken down into a variety of smaller units but avowing its integrity at each stage by its very title of integer. To manipulate pure numbers in the brain is, however, a rather severe test of mental powers. It is only for a few people with mathematical idiosyncrasies (i.e. those who find in numbers their own apt and proper toys), that mental arithmetic is an enjoyable occupation. Apart from purely mathematical puzzles, I know of only one wholly mental number game commonly played by children, that one which begins, 'Think of a number, double it', etc. In all the important and widespread number games the numbers are wedded to things, to small objects which can be handled, such as dominoes, dice and playing cards. In such cases a connection between objects of thought and objects of sense is created, the better to satisfy the game's demand for tangible units of manipulation. A psychologist puts this point clearly when he says that in cards and chess the player handles the objects of thought (H. L. Hollingworth, *The Psychology of Thought*, p.110). In cards the pasteboard units bear a number. Chess, though a similar case, has pieces which stand not for numbers but for something much nearer the elements of logic, particular sets of relations, each piece representing a specified force in a particular relation to the other forces similarly represented on the board. It was Alekhin, the great chess-player, who said that he saw the pieces in his mind as force-symbols, in so far as the process could be put into words.[1] It is well known

[1] Quoted by Graham Wallas, *The Art of Thought*, p. 72.

that the great chess masters are capable of playing entirely in the abstract, conducting a number of games simultaneously while seeing none of them. This is admittedly a rather special case, for at this point the game is becoming so abstract and refined that it seems to be leaving the world of play altogether and taking to that of logistic. For ordinary players, however, the chessmen are there on the board to represent the connecting points of the system of relations involved.

 We come now to language and to games with words and things. It is obvious that games can be played with things alone, with a jigsaw puzzle for instance, and the most elementary forms of word-and-thing games are those where language is employed merely as an auxiliary to assist the attention or memory, and the emphasis is on things rather than words. Games of this type are 'Kim's Game', where the player has to observe a random collection of small objects for a fixed length of time and then write down their names from memory; or the game of 'I spy with my little eye', where a particular feature of language—the fact that words begin with a certain letter— is used to narrow the field of things from which the guess must be made. Another memory game which employs words as a medium is 'My grandmother went to market and she bought . . .' where each player adds the name of a new object but has first to remember in the right order all the other objects already contributed to the list. This is a purely mental game (it is one of the useful games that can be played in the dark) and it could presumably have taken the form of remembering a list of numbers, if the memory were the real focus of interest. Games, however, are interested in objects and in real life, and so the memory test takes the form of a list of words referring to things, though the latter will be strangely assorted. This is true of another memory game, The Parson's Cat. In this game each player in turn has to supply a different epithet for the cat, the epithet to begin with a given letter. It is really a test of vocabulary and memory, since what the game really does is to see who can think of the longest list of adjectives beginning with C, let us say. It does not take that form, however; on the contrary, a real thing is introduced, a cat, with a series of extravagant properties. It will be in the course of the game a clever cat, a cautious cat, a crimson cat and so on, but a cat always; and there is even a wholly gratuitous parson thrown in as well. The same thing applies to 'I love my love with an H', which also is a vocabulary test linked to an image, dealing in nouns and adjectives and a concrete situation. The game 'When Suddenly . . .' is similarly concerned with an unexpected series of things and happenings called up by words. One player begins a story and ends his short contribution with the formula 'when suddenly', at which point the next player has to take it on, add to it as best he can and pass it on to the next player in the same way. There is an excellent example of the game in Chapter 12 of Louisa Alcott's *Little Women*. The game of Consequences follows the same lines, and is too familiar to need explanation. This game starts with names, selected independently by the different players. The point of the game is that some incongruous unity should arise from the multiplicity of choices made by a number of minds, and unless the names given convey a reference that is familiar (no matter at what level of experience) to all the players, the game will fail of its purpose. If it produces the Prime Minister meeting Little Red Ridinghood in Heaven, all will be well; but if two names taken at random from a telephone directory and the name of an obscure village were to be substituted, the game would not work, because the connection between the words and familiar units of experience would not have been made.

These are examples where the mind is playing with a series of references to things, or to properties of things, as they appear in everyday life. This is made possible by the fact that language attaches a certain fixed group of letters and sounds to a certain reference. The word makes an apparently simple unit out of some fact which, if looked at in itself, will almost certainly be highly complex, and in this way it is possible to play with a series of references, since the words attached to them keep them mentally distinct. The process works both ways, for if the word keeps the reference distinct as a unit, it is thanks to the attached reference that the group of sounds and letters constitutes a word at all. Words are themselves units made up of collections of smaller units, the twenty-six letters of the alphabet, and play with these lesser units is possible as well. The individual letters can be disordered and rearranged, as in anagrams or word-building games played with letter-cards. There is an interesting point to be noticed about all games of this type. They do not depend merely upon the possibility of arranging series of letters in various ways. They turn upon the fact that certain combinations of letters bear reference, i.e. form a *word*, and the object of the game is always directed towards such a group. The result of the building or reshuffling has to be a word and not gibberish which is a group of letters to which no unit of reference is attached. The object of the game is not to disorder a given order, not to produce one disorder out of another; it is to rearrange a given disordered series of letter units, forming in themselves no final unit for the mind because the memory attaches to them no reference in experience, into a series which can be regarded as a unit in its own right since it will refer to something in experience and so form, in language convention, a word.

This type of game with words has many variations. I give four examples with which I am familiar. (I have drawn on my own memory for the games in this chapter. It would of course have been possible to consult some manual on the subject of word-games, but we need be concerned here only with the simple and normal ones, and I assume that one memory is as good a repository of these as any other.)

(1) The Conundrum or Enigma, in which the player, with the help of rhyming clues, must select from certain given words a series of letters, one at a time, which will eventually build up a word with a given meaning.

(2) Two or more players each say a letter in turn. This series of letters must build up a word, but the aim of each player is not to end a word but to prolong it so that another player will have to end it and so forfeit a point. Each player must, however, have a specific word in mind each time he adds a letter, and can be challenged on this.

(3) Each of two or more players starts with a small empty crossword puzzle frame, five squares by five. Each says a letter in turn, and the aim is to build up as many and as long words as possible within the frame, by placing in it, in order, the letters of one's own choice and those chosen by the other players.

(4) Two words are proposed, of the same length: and the puzzle consists in linking these together by interposing other words, each of which shall differ from the next word in one letter only. That is to say, one letter may be changed in one of the given words, then one letter in the word so obtained and so on, till we arrive at the other given word. The letters must not be interchanged among themselves, but each must keep to its own place. As an example, the word 'head' may be changed into 'tail' by interposing the words 'heal, teal, tell, tall, tail.' (*Note:* This game, called Doublets, appears to have been invented by Lewis Carroll, and it is his explanation of it, from the March number of *Vanity Fair*, 1879, which is given above.)

The game in each of these cases is to manipulate the letter units so as to obtain a given word unit. The letters are units for play only in so far as they contribute towards this result. The mind, in fact, is not interested in playing with the twenty-six letters as such; it is interested in making them into groups which shall refer to experience.

So far we have been looking at the mind playing with words as reference units or with combinations of letters which, if successfully manipulated, yield words. There are other cases, however, where a group of letters or sounds does a double duty, carrying two or more references.

> The Llama of the pampases you never should confound,
> Despite a most deceptive similarity of sound,
> With the Lama who is lord of Turkestan.
>
> (BELLOC)

Games can be played on this type of duality, the picture puzzles, for instance, where the player when confronted with the drawing of a boat's sail, let us say, has to interpret it as sale if he is to build up the required message. It may be just a similarity of look, as in the bows of a ship and the bows on a child's hair. Or it may be that an identical group covers two or more completely distinct references, a group such as *port* for instance; and so we come to the pun which obviously belongs here since it is said to be a play upon words. Upon these double references depend most riddles and the more complex crossword clues and acrostics, where spatial intersection of particular words is added to the game. Simpler crosswords depend on homonyms, where one reference may have two possible word expressions such as 'beneath' and 'under' or 'almost' and 'nearly'.

The objects being played with here are a little more complicated, but the nature of the complication must be understood. Even with puns, the mind is still on safe ground, moving among clearly defined units. The element of chance in a language produces this type of material, but this does not mean that the playthings are unreliable, even if some of them, as in the case of puns, come two in a box. This is where a pun differs from an ambiguity, as Mr. Empson has pointed out. Speaking of the nineteenth-century punster, he says, 'he uses puns to break away from the echoes and implications of words, to distract your attention by insisting on his ingenuity so that you can escape from sinking into the meaning' (*Seven Types of Am-*

biguity, Chatto & Windus, London, 1947, revised edition, Ch. III, p. 109.)[1] If this is so, it is an interesting comment on Carroll's continual punning in the Alices. A pun is not simple but it is not ambiguous. It is of the very nature of the pun that its meanings are separate, and are therefore still within the mind's control.

Things and words in everyday life are regarded by the thinking or playing mind as safe, distinct and manageable. This is true of numbers as well; in fact, they are safer than things, or words which refer to things, because they are less subject to chance. This sense of certainty is all-important in thinking or playing. We feel certain of numbers, and of words and things in so far as they resemble numbers in being separate units. Word games go as far as they can in treating words in this way, as if they were things, as children do who 'play with words as they do with sand or blocks' (Karl Groos, *The Play of Man*, p. 142). Both prose and play demand this type of certainty, but since it turns upon the integrity and distinctness of the units it is a very precarious one where language is concerned. The groups of letters forming the words seem stable enough, but reference is bound to be variable, even if only within certain limits. This introduces a traitor into the camp at once, for something that is widely variable cannot be played with. It is at this point that the dream element begins to creep into language; and in dreams, and still more in nightmare, things are not separate and controllable and the mind cannot play with them. Dream vision is essentially fluid; nothing is reliable, anything may change into anything else, our comfortably numbered time foreshortens into simultaneity, a thing may be two things, or a person two people, at the same moment. The result is that dreams cannot be controlled and so cannot be played with. From this something rather alarming seems to

[1] Cf. G. K. Chesterton, *The Victorian Age in Literature*, Ch. III, p. 172, 'In Browning the word with two meanings seems to mean rather less, if anything, than the word with one.'

follow: that dreams play with the dreamer, who is ourself. Perhaps this holds good of all the things in experience which we cannot break down and control and play with. They may play with us.

It can already be seen how this concerns the Alices. It may seem strange to say that Nonsense is a game and that games are hostile to the dream, for both the Alices are set in dream form. Critics have in fact emphasized a connection between Nonsense and dreams. M. Cammaerts says that the world of Nonsense is not so much Fairyland as Dreamland (*op. cit.*, p. 32). Another speaks of 'that best book of dreams, *Alice in Wonderland*' (H. G. Hutchinson, *Dreams and their Meanings*, Longmans, Green, London, 1901, Ch. IV, p. 75). Mr. De La Mare gives Nonsense for its setting 'a state . . . of life to which we most of us win admittance only when we are blessedly asleep' (*op. cit.*, p. 60). Mr. Empson says in *Some Versions of the Pastoral* that 'the rhymes affect one as conventions of the dream world, and this sets the tone about conventions' (p. 290). He says elsewhere, of the nineteenth century, 'This cult of vagueness produced the nonsense writers like Lear and Lewis Carroll' (*Seven Types of Ambiguity*, p. 187).

The general view of Nonsense is that it creates disorder out of order as a dream does:—

> Hey diddle diddle, the cat and the fiddle,
> The cow jumped over the moon.

> We're all in the dumps
> For Diamonds are trumps,
> The kittens have gone to Saint Pauls,
> The babies are bit,
> The moon's in a fit
> And the houses are built without walls.

> There was an old man on the Border,
> Who lived in the utmost disorder;
> He danced with the cat, and made tea in his hat,
> Which vexed all the folks on the Border.
>
> (LEAR, M.N.)

Then fill up the glasses with treacle and ink,
And anything else that is pleasant to drink.
(*Queen Alice*, T.L.G.)

This certainly looks like disorder, as if the writer had put
a spoon into the remembered stuff of our normal solid
universe and given it a good stir. But of what nature is
this disorder? The words, as groups of letters and sounds,
are not disordered. In certain cases Nonsense does embark
on private manipulations and creations of word units, producing such results as the Jabberwock vocabulary, and
this will have to be looked into; but on the whole, as in the
examples above, it employs familiar words. The syntax
and grammar are not disordered. Carroll was enough of a
stickler for exactitude in these matters to insist that his
printers use the form 'ca'n't' and 'sha'n't' and 'wo'n't'
instead of the usually accepted, if more slipshod, forms.
Mr. De La Mare says of him 'he was a precisian. If any
one even of his little girls slipped in her grammar when
writing to him he corrected it in his reply' (*Lewis Carroll*,
p. 24). It is noticeable, too, how often Nonsense takes the
form of verse, which by its organization is the reverse of
disordered. There is only one aspect of language which
Nonsense can be said to disorder, and that is reference, the
effect produced by a word or group of words in the mind.
It is the sequence of references which is disordered by
Nonsense, if the familiar sequence of events in everyday
life is to be taken as the standard of order and sense.

As we saw earlier, it is important to keep the distinction
between words and things. Nonsense does not attempt to
disorder the things themselves. If it did, if it attempted
to affect the normal order of things in real life by the use
of words, it would step straight out of the world of Nonsense into that of magic. M. Cammaerts, in *The Poetry of
Nonsense*, p. 30, remarks on the inadmissibility of magic in
Nonsense. There is only one instance in Lear of something
being turned into something else. It is in the *Four Little
Children*: 'they proceeded to make tea . . . but as they had

no tea-leaves, they merely placed some pebbles in the hot
water, and the Quangle-Wangle played some tunes over
it on an Accordion, by which of course tea was made
directly, and of the very best quality.' The 'of course' in
that last sentence is a curious touch, ironically adult and
safeguarding. One Nursery Rhyme comes somewhere near
the point, only to withdraw from it again, the Old Woman
who went to market and fell asleep on the way home:—

> There came by a pedlar whose name was Stout,
> He cut her petticoats round about;
> He cut her petticoats up to her knees
> Which made the little woman to shiver and sneeze.

> When this little woman first did wake,
> She began to shiver and she began to shake;
> She began to shake and she began to cry,
> 'Lauk a mercy on me, this is none of I!'

The fear of some change in the integrity of the individual
is plainly there. Early in Wonderland we meet a similar
conflict in the heroine's mind: 'Her eyes filled with tears
again as she went on, "I must be Mabel after all." ' Once
in Wonderland and once in the Looking-Glass things start
turning into other things. In the latter it is the shop scene,
where the White Queen becomes a sheep, knitting needles
turn into oars and the shop into a stream. It is an interesting chapter because it seems to break all the rules, so
much so that in atmosphere it comes uncomfortably near
the point at the end of the book where Queen Alice's feast
suddenly becomes completely unstable, and Alice has to
wake up. We shall come back to this later, but at present
we need only notice that in *Wool and Water* Alice is 'half
surprised and half frightened' at the changes, and I believe
this slight sense of uneasiness is shared by the readers of
this particular chapter. In Wonderland the creature that
turns into something else is the Duchess's baby. While
Alice is carrying it, it starts turning into a pig, and Alice
indicates her own reserve at this proceeding: 'If you're

D

going to turn into a pig, my dear, I'll have nothing more to do with you.' In the Mad Gardener's song, scattered verse by verse through the two parts of *Sylvie and Bruno*, something turns into something else in each verse; but even here, though the gardener is admitted to be mad, the same attitude of reserve and gloom and suspicion prevails towards these transformations, in six out of the nine verses Carroll wrote. I give two examples, but each verse follows the same pattern, the first four lines giving the change-over and the last two the comment on it:—

> He thought he saw an Elephant
>   That practised on a fife:
> He looked again, and found it was
>   A letter from his wife.
> 'At length I realize,' he said,
>   'The bitterness of life.'

> He thought he saw an Argument
>   That proved he was the Pope:
> He looked again, and found it was
>   A Bar of Mottled Soap.
> 'A fact so dread,' he faintly said,
>   'Extinguishes all hope.'

The Snark produces disappearances and transformations, but these are not the true stuff of Nonsense, and the Gardener and Alice are right in their reaction towards such happenings. Magic would disrupt Nonsense because it allows the notion of substitutions and co-existences, of one thing disappearing or turning into another. This type of disorder, however, is typical not only of magic but of dream as well, with its extension into nightmare and delusion; and that is why I said earlier that Nonsense is hostile to the dream. It is important to differentiate between this type of disorder, fluidity, the synthesis, the running together of pictures in the mind, and the type with which Nonsense works and which we have tentatively called a rearrangement in the series of word references. Throughout this work the term 'disorder' will mean the first type, that of dream and madness. If we are right, the second is not disorder so much as a condition necessary for the playing of a game.

Dream and game meet particularly clearly at one point in Wonderland, when Alice is trying to play croquet. She finds the game very troublesome because the objects with which it is played are only partially under her control and refuse to remain quiet and biddable. They have the mobility of dreams, and are characteristic dream substitutions. Instead of a mallet she has a flamingo, instead of a ball a hedgehog and instead of a hoop a soldier. This suggests that the only really safe things, the reliable unchanging things suitable for play, are dead. If Nonsense is itself a game, this becomes rather sinister, and may begin to explain why the Queen of Hearts keeps shouting 'Off with his head!' and why, according to Mr. Empson's view, the fear of death is one of the crucial topics of these books (*Some Versions of the Pastoral*, p. 291).

We could follow either of these two threads, the Dream or the Game, through the Alices and Nonsense. The dream element in the croquet upsets the game, and it seems better to concentrate on what appears the more characteristic activity rather than on the intrusion; but the point to realize is that either would be possible, and in the end they would probably come to the same thing. We are merely making a choice in a matter of dialectic— or call it a game—deciding to throw in our lot on the side of Nonsense-as-a-Game rather than on the side of Nonsense-as-a-Dream. It may seem perverse to emphasize the feasibility of the contrary argument, but to do so is literally half the battle. Exercises in dialectic, like games, have nothing to do with such a notion as 'truth'. We shall not find out the truth about Nonsense, any more than we should if we were to follow the contrary argument, or both at once. Perhaps there is no truth to find out, any more than there would be in a nightmare or a game of chess, the notion being out of place.

This situation raises one question, however, which is as important as it is difficult to answer and which is thrown up by dream and game alike : who is playing, or who is dreaming? In the Looking-Glass we are left with the unresolved problem whether the narrative recorded was Alice's dream or the Red King's dream. That question can be asked not merely about the dream but about the game which gives the book its framework. Who was playing it? It is clear that Alice is not so much playing as being played with. 'Her companion only smiled pleasantly, and said, "That's easily managed. You can be the White Queen's pawn, if you like, as Lily's too young to play" ' (*The Garden of Live Flowers*). If Alice is a pawn, someone else is playing with her. We can leave the dream problem alone; but if Nonsense is a game, we still have to find out who is the player.

It would be so simple if we could say it is the Nonsense writer, and leave it at that; but that would be a most doubtful answer. In analysing Nonsense, or poetry, or any other system, one can work out for oneself a form of systematics of the particular construction, but it is practically certain that the poet or constructor was unaware of systematics while making his construction. Yet this need not disqualify the systematics as a way of thinking about the construction or the constructor's mind. The difficulty is that any enquiry into a system is an enquiry into the mind which makes systems, and that is any mind, examiner or examinee, object or subject. I do not want to suggest that Lear and Carroll knew they were playing a game. All we need at the moment is the suggestion that Nonsense can be looked at as if it were a game. We will play our own game on those terms, and hope to see in time who plays the game—Lear, Carroll, the reader of Nonsense, the mind enquiring into Nonsense processes, or perhaps all of these together. A mind may play with itself, forming its own internal dialectic from time to time, each momentary half playing with the other. We will concentrate on this interplay for the present rather than on the question whether the individual is conscious of it or not. Individual, however, there certainly is, the undivided mind, although we may think of it in halves; and that one mind may be anybody's. This is why the game or the dream, logic or irrationality, may lead us to the same point in the end, and why we shall not come anywhere near the answer to the problem until we reach that point in our own minds, which we shall probably do, as Lear and Carroll may have done, without knowing it.

Chapter 5

ONE AND ONE AND ONE AND ONE AND ONE

IF NONSENSE is not created by the principle of disorder in the mind, and if it is not that resolution of order
and disorder in the field of language which is poetry, there
is only one thing left which it can be, and at first sight this
is disconcerting. For the only thing left is the mind's force
towards order.

There are two things that are going to be helpful in
the slightly topsy-turvy situation we have now reached.
The first is to remember the precision, the delight in
number and logic, the interest in meticulous and well-
ordered detail which characterized the minds of Lear and
Carroll. They were not compelled to be like that. There
was presumably no external reason why Carroll, or perhaps one should say Dodgson, chose to specialize in
mathematics and logic, or why Lear chose to keep minute
records of the details of ordinary life; presumably each
enjoyed doing so. Carroll's propensities in this direction
are well known, his file of correspondence, for instance, in
which he recorded and summarized all incoming and out-
going letters over a period of thirty-seven years, so that
by the time he died there were 98,000 cross-references in
his files. It is interesting that Lear's character should have
been so similar. He said of himself that he had a 'tendency
to an analytical state of mind'.[1] It seems probable that
each man's art of Nonsense was founded upon a similar
brand of enjoyment. And what each enjoyed was order.

The second thing that will be helpful is the view and
definition of art given in Scholastic philosophy. We have
met St. Thomas Aquinas already, and we are likely to go

[1] Letter to Chichester Fortescue, January 3rd, 1858.

on meeting him as we proceed, for the Schoolmen seem to be the only people who can help in this enquiry into Nonsense, just because they are so logical. I cannot claim to be an expert in this field, but equally I cannot wait to complete this study until I am one, so we shall go along here very simply, piece by piece, and I will give chapter and verse for the arguments involved. One's own inexperience, however, does not mean that this is not a right and proper place from which to seek assistance. The conjunction of Scholasticism and Nonsense is not a piece of whimsy and has been made by others beside myself. Harry Morgan Ayres in *Carroll's Alice*, (pp. 18 and 53), says of Carroll, 'He would have made a great Schoolman . . . It is no child's tale that was there begun, it is a *summa* of human experience in its disillusioning quest for wisdom.' So to the Schoolmen and the *Summa* we go.

We may start with two quotations. The first is from St. Thomas, 'the giving form to a work of art is by means of the form of the art in the mind of the artist' (*Summa Theologica*, Pt. I, Q. 74, Art. 3). The second is from Maritain's *Art and Scholasticism*, p. 9 ff., where he summarizes the teaching of the Schoolmen upon art:—

> Art is before all intellectual, and its activity consists in impressing an idea upon a matter: therefore it resides in the mind of the *artifex*, or, as they say, it is subject in that mind. . . . For the work in hand to turn out well, there must correspond to it in the soul of the workman such a disposition as will produce between them a sort of congruence and intimate proportion which the Schoolmen termed *connaturality* . . . Through the presence in them of the virtue of Art, they *are*, in a way, their work before they create it: to be able to form it, they have conformed to it.

If we take these side by side, it seems not utterly incongruous to suggest order as the principle of organization in Nonsense. The minds of these two Nonsense writers were orderly, and if the work of art is connatural with the mind of the artist, then Nonsense may be orderly too. Obviously, it cannot be complete order. For one thing, common sense tells us that the Nonsense world is otherwise ordered than that of everyday. For another, Nonsense is made of words, and words are, in part at least, subject to disorder in the mind. If Nonsense is on the side of order, what does it do about disorder?

We have come back to the phraseology of play again when we speak of Nonsense being on the side of order. Disorder is on the opposite side, the opponent to be played against. This characterisitc of tension or struggle is regarded by some writers on the subject as one of the basic characteristics of play. If dialectic belongs to the nature of play, this particular case of it, the order–disorder dialectic in the mind, may be the defining characteristic of the game of Nonsense. It is perhaps necessary to point out that dialectic does not require two actually separate minds for its operation. One mind that can diversify itself for the purposes of argument or play will be sufficient. One recalls that Carroll says of his heroine, 'once she remembered trying to box her own ears for having cheated herself in a game of croquet she was playing against herself, for this curious child was very fond of pretending to be two people' (*Down the Rabbit-Hole*, A.A.W.). If the two forces of order and disorder in the mind form the two poles of the dialectic in the Nonsense game, a distinction between Nonsense and poetry at once becomes possible, for poetry aims at an equilibrium, even if only momentary, between the two forces, an enchanted instant of reconciliation; whereas Nonsense is going to be a battle, with our lot thrown in on one side and all available energy directed towards keeping the opponent in play, lest he in turn seize the initiative and establish control. (Binet says that this element of battle is what distinguishes chess thought from mathematical thought, *Psychologie des Grands Calculateurs et Joueurs d'Echecs*, Pt. II, Ch. II, p. 229.)

The battle in Nonsense is bound to be inconclusive, because so long as the mind stays in the field of language, to which Nonsense is limited, it cannot suppress the force towards disorder in the mind, nor defeat it conclusively, for this force is essential to the mind no less than the opposing force of order. Nonsense can only engage the force towards disorder in continual play. This is true of dialectic itself: it has no end. Both the Alices end arbitrarily; there seems no very good reason why the story should finish at just that point rather than any other. The three battles recorded in *Through the Looking-Glass* have similar endings. The Tweedledum and Tweedledee fight, which in fact never comes off, is arranged on the basis of 'Let's fight till six and then have dinner' (*Tweedledum and Tweedledee*, T.L.G.). The next fight, that of the Lion and the Unicorn, has already reached an advanced stage by the time the reader arrives; 'each of them has been down about eighty-seven times', and it seems as if the fight is never going to end.

> At this moment the Unicorn sauntered by them, with his hands in his pockets. 'I had the best of it this time?' he said to the King, just glancing at him as he passed.
> 'A little, a little,' the King replied, rather nervously.

Indeed, Alice's suggestion that a conclusion would be in order is scouted:—

> 'Does—the one—that wins—get the crown?' she asked, as well as she could, for the run was putting her quite out of breath.
> 'Dear me, no!' said the King. 'What an idea!'
> (*The Lion and the Unicorn*, T.L.G.)

The last fight in the book, that between the White and the Red Knight, follows the same pattern:—

> Another Rule of Battle, that Alice had not noticed, seemed to be that they always fell on their heads; and the battle ended with their both falling off in this way, side by side. When they got up again, they shook hands, and then the Red Knight mounted and galloped off.

'It was a glorious victory, wasn't it?' said the White
Knight, as he came up panting.

'I don't know', Alice said doubtfully.

('*It's My Own Invention*', T.L.G.)

The game of Nonsense may, then, consist in the mind's
employing its tendency towards order to engage its contrary tendency towards disorder, keeping the latter perpetually in play and so in check. The apparent disorder
in the Nonsense world may be the result of such an
encounter.

The next thing is to discover the nature of the side we
are playing on and playing against. It has already been
suggested that order in the mind tends in the direction of
number and logic, while disorder moves towards dream
and nightmare. The investigation of the two forces will
probably be best begun at the two extremes.

We will begin with order, and logic. Logic is the science
of relation in the abstract. The nature of the terms con-
stituting the intersection points or meeting-places of those
relations is of no importance; only the relations matter.
The terms can be words, symbols, numbers, letters. If
words are used they will, by virtue of the fact that they
are words, have some reference to experience, but that
reference is irrelevant to the construction of the logic. It
does not matter of what nature the terms are that are to
be related; but terms there must be, and *terms* in the plural,
for relations cannot be established or manipulated between
a nothing and a nothing, so to speak. 'Every relation must
have terms in order to become visible to the understanding
at all' (Susanne K. Langer, *An Introduction to Symbolic
Logic*, Ch. II, p. 49). Equally you cannot establish relations and a logic where there is only one term; if everything were all one, the only relation that could be
established would be self-identity, and that does not get
one very far. So we come to the conclusion that 'every real
relation requires and implies in reality two terms' (*Summa*,
Pt. I, Q. 28, Art. 1) and those two must be distinguishable

from one another. They need not be simple—no words are simple, for instance—but one property they must have: each term in the collection must be such that the mind can distinguish it from the other terms. Logic requires for its operation a collection of discrete units, and the nature of the mind's operation in logic consists in attending to certain relations existing, or considered as existing, between those terms.

So far so good; but when we turn to nightmare and try to formulate the nature of the mind's operation under the influence of disorder, we are at once in difficulties, for we have no proper instrument for this side of the investigation. Nightmare, and to a lesser extent dream, are the opposite of logic, but the mind can only think logically if it is to think consciously and rationally at all. It knows of no other way of constructing its thought, and to use it on dream activity is like trying to open a tin can with a pair of scissors. If only we knew how to employ this force towards disorder we could perhaps find a method which would fit this field; but we have not found it yet, or perhaps have forgotten it many centuries ago, and so we have to make shift here with logic, inappropriate though it is. Its uselessness lies in what we have just seen: that it requires for its operation the existence of a class of distinct terms. This is just exactly what nightmare cannot provide. In the dream system it is impossible to distinguish units of thought. This is not to be regarded as a weakness or deficiency in the system itself. It is only the one-sidedness of our minds, trained to respect logic and dismiss nightmare, which makes us feel that any system ought to require units for its working, and that nightmare is somehow inferior to logic because it does not. The point is that this system works on other principles, and we have to try to make our minds conceive consciously (there is no difficulty in apprehending such a thing at the unconscious level) of a system where the aim is to establish all possible relations without distinguishing terms. In one particular, logic and nightmare are alike, for in neither system is the nature of the material of any importance. Logic attends to a minimum of select relations between distinct terms and eliminates chance by the precision and control of the system. Nightmare swamps chance by doing the opposite, attending simultaneously to all possible relations so that the system can in this way include anything and everything that the mind can produce, the jumble of memories, impressions and bodily sensations which form the raw material of dream and nightmare. The elements of this material cannot be isolated from one another. The continuous flux and transformation of the dream is not, however, incoherent; its aim is coherence, total and all-embracing, but of its own kind. When the process reaches its culmination we pass into an all-inclusive universe of everythingness where nothing happens by chance because everything is related to everything else in a multiplicity of ways. Compare the picture Piaget gives of the normal thought-world of the child, 'For him, everything is connected with everything else, which comes to exactly the same thing as that nothing is connected with anything else' (*Judgment and Reasoning in the Child*, p. 61.)

Where it is impossible to distinguish units one cannot decide what comes before what, and thus the establishment of serial order, which turns upon the notion of 'preceding' and 'following', becomes impossible, with consequent dislocation in dreams of such series in waking experience as space, time and causation. Dunne explains this feature of dreams in terms of a new time-theory, while Whitehead links it with the theory of relativity and the space-time concept;[1] but we need only observe that in this, for our purposes, seems to lie the essential distinguishing mark between order and disorder in the mind. Order operates with units, disorder without. The conditions of operation of both systems are mental and, in the true sense of the word, artificial. Reality, as we may judge it from ex-

---

[1] *Vide* J. W. Dunne, *An Experiment with Time* and *The Serial Universe*, and Alfred North Whitehead, *Essay in Science and Philosophy*.

perience, presents itself to us under both forms, unitary and non-unitary, successive and simultaneous; but the distinction we are making between these two ways of working lies not in their relation to reality, but in what use each makes of this idea of Oneness. For although nightmare does not operate with ones or units, it does not discard the idea of oneness altogether: it tries to run everything into one. So logic begins with one and one and one, nightmare ends with one big One.

The fact that logic has to have units or ones at its disposal and builds from these a construction means that every logical whole can always be resolved into its parts again. The finished construction may be regarded as a whole, as one, but it must always be capable of being broken down into parts. Nightmare on the other hand ends with the idea of one, and ends with it so emphatically that everything has become one in the perfected system. This oneness is utterly unlike the oneness of logic either at the beginning or end of the latter's operation, since the oneness of nightmare is irreversible; it cannot be resolved into its component parts because it never had any distinguishable parts in the first place.[1] At this stage the problem is threatening to land us in deep waters, extra-territorial waters if I may use the phrase; for this looks like the old theme of analysis and synthesis, of a whole and its parts, of particulars and generals, unity and variety. We had better stick to something simpler, the difference noted so far between the two forces of order and disorder as regards the use made of the concept of One. (I do not propose to attempt any definition of One, but shall take it as a self-evident concept.) Order in the mind demands a number of ones at the beginning of its operation, disorder demands a complete oneness at the end.

In logic and nightmare, the mind is operating on itself and is therefore of necessity isolated. When the mind

[1] Cf. Piaget on the reversibility of logic and the irreversibility of non-directed thought, *op. cit.*, pp. 171–2.

moves more into the centre of operations, the field of language, it comes back to a point where communication and a sense of the reality of the natural world are possible, because language by the fact of reference connects the mind with experience, and it is at this level that we can establish contact with other minds. In logic and nightmare, the mind is working in systems which do not have this connection with language and experience, and so it loses its sense of reality and the means of communication. In nightmare the force towards disorder seeks to make everything into one, including the mind, and so at last the mind can no longer operate since it has become one with what is being operated upon. This is interesting because it suggests a reason for that fearful sense of impotence and imprisonment which is a common feature of nightmare. The characteristic operation of nightmare reaches its term in this total oneness where operation ceases to be possible, since operator and operation are one, and the detachment necessary for control has disappeared. The same thing is true, in its own way, of logic as well. In logic the mind starts with a collection of ones upon which it is to operate; but since it is concerned with pure relation, these ones may have no content beyond the fact of their oneness, and while operating on them the mind encloses itself in a universe of pure abstract form and becomes a tissue of relations. Apart from the crossing-places of the relation-lines it can, in strict logic, have nothing, and the result may be that the mind has the sense of vanishing itself.

We seem to have come a long way from the idea of a game, for at each end of these two systems, logic and nightmare, the respective infinities of nothingness and everythingness wait to swallow up the mind, and this is no game; or if it is, it is a dangerous one for the mind to play. Normally the mind ventures only briefly into either system, some minds perhaps not at all. The two neighbouring systems of number and dream, which lead the mind back towards language, are less extreme and much

more familiar, and we had better consider them for a
moment in connection with this notion of Oneness. Dream,
the halfway house of disorder in the mind, runs its material
together, making curious unions and analogies; but—and
this is where I would draw the dividing line between
dream on the one hand and nightmare and hallucination
on the other—it leaves the total mind still in possession of
its sense of personality and detachment. It does not impair
the integrity of the individual. The dreamer can still wake
up and say with Bunyan, 'I awoke and behold it was a
dream.' The dream tends towards oneness but the mind is
separate from the process and can, on waking, set the
dream into words, thereby establishing a measure of control over it and communicating it to other minds. The
same thing happens with number, the halfway house of
order. Number is applicable to reality and is in the control
of the mind, which manipulates it and applies it to reality,
but as a separate instrument which does not affect the
mind's conviction of its own identity. Perhaps it is the
mind's need to preserve this sense of identity and of separation from the number system which makes the human personality react so strongly against any situation where it is
given a number instead of a name, where in fact it has
been forcibly identified with its own instrument and so has
become a cipher.

It has taken us a long time to come back to the middle
field of language, where words, and the game with words
which is Nonsense, belong. We have cleared the ground,
however, for if the game of Nonsense takes the side of order
and plays against disorder in the mind, we now have some
idea what that implies. Nonsense will presumably have to
organize its language according to the principles of order,
i.e. it will have to concentrate on the divisibility of its
material into ones, units from which a universe can be
built. This universe, however, must never be more than
the sum of its parts, and must never fuse into some all-
embracing whole which cannot be broken down again

into the original ones. It must try to create with words a universe that consists of bits. This is where the title of this chapter comes in. In *Queen Alice* in *Through the Looking-Glass* the White Queen asks, 'What's one and one and one and one and one and one and one and one and one and one?' Alice cannot answer, and that is not just accident. The point is that the sum-total is unimportant; it is the composition of it that matters, for this is to be the composition of the universe of Nonsense, a collection of ones which can be summed together into a whole but which can always fall back into separate ones again. This is one half of the game. The other half will be to see that the mind retains its sense of separateness from whatever is being manipulated, and it all has to be done with words.

Chapter 6

CONCRETE AND FASTIDIOUS

THE FIELD of the Nonsense game is language, so that in theory the game could be played with the whole of language. Games, however, demand enclosure, limitation and rules. Their nature requires that they must be rigidly limited in field and methods if they are to function freely, and it follows that Nonsense will have to draw its own limitations in order to protect its freedom and function. Since Nonsense consists of words, this limitation can be achieved in one way only, the selection and arrangement of words.

It is important to be clear about this, for in this fact lies the difficulty of the Nonsense writer's task. He cannot abandon words, as the mathematician and the musician can do, for some more controllable means of communication. Neither can he suppress the force towards disorder which any mind, including his own, possesses. The difficulty of controlling words lies in the variability of the reference in language. The variability is not unlimited, or there could be no communication at all; but no writer can wholly prevent or control the personal associations and variations which the use of a particular word will set moving in another mind. All he can do is to attempt, by the selection and arrangement of his words, to keep the attention of that other mind fixed as far as possible in a certain direction, according to the purpose that the writer has in mind, and so prevent it wandering off into that private inconsequence which is the normal state of the mind when its attention is not engaged. The more precise and orderly the writer's aim, the more careful he will have to be in the choice and organization of his words, as any philosopher or poet or scientist knows.

If we are right so far, the aim of Nonsense is very precise indeed. It is by means of language to set before the mind a possible universe in which everything goes along serially, by one and one. This serial order must not be upset by indistinctness of the units or by fusion of the whole. This means that the force towards disorder in the mind must be inhibited, both as regards the mind's tendency to produce and develop trains of dreamlike and personal associations in connection with words and phrases, and as regards its tendency to run collections of such images together into some new unity. The original references must not develop, and there must be no final manifold. The aim, an essential one if the conditions for play are to be fulfilled, is the preservation of distinctness, each unit a distinct one, as each chess piece of any importance is distinct from its fellows, and the whole a collection of distinct parts. The problem resolves itself at this stage into a juggling with the notions of singularity and plurality, but—and this is the difficulty and fascination of the game—in a medium where it is not easy to distinguish between them. Words regarded as letters and sounds apparently present no problem, for we know roughly what is one word and what is more than one; but in the case of reference the distinction is far less easy to make. The mind is a muddle in this respect, a fruitful muddle perhaps but a muddle none the less.

It is this that makes the job of thinking about reference in words so difficult, and a classification of it almost impossible. We must, however, attempt something of the sort if we are to see what variations the Nonsense writer is faced with, and what he can make his selection from. It is possible to divide up words very roughly according to the extent to which their content appears to be a stable unit or a variable in the mind. First come words which convey a single precise reference to the mind, without any diversity or muddle at all. There are not many of these, the principal examples being technical terms and words of number. The second group consists of words which refer to the facts of sense perception and the normal content of experience. There is a certain diversity here, owing to variations in individual experience, but not so great a variety as to overcome the unity of the reference as a whole. In the third group are words conveying a reference which for ordinary minds is vague and ill-defined; such words are usually abstract rather than concrete, and may convey very different references to different minds. Once again the word provides just enough unity for some reference to be conveyed, but the variety is more evident than the unity, and indistinctness is the result. One other group must be mentioned here, which although it does not belong in the field of normal language will concern us in due course. These are the Nonsense words which convey no apparent reference at all and are coined by Nonsense writers for their own purposes. They may look as if they belong in a different class altogether, a kind of null-class, incapable of being classified according to a unity-variety balance in the content. I believe, however, that this is not so, and that they may turn out to be in the direct line of succession of Groups One to Three above, representing unlimited diversity with no unity other than that imposed by a particular collection of letters and sounds. If so, they will complete the range from unity to plurality.

Words looked at in this way carry within themselves their own contribution to the Nonsense writer's problem of handling unity and diversity in the mind, and that writer will have to take this into account. It should be possible to see how the words used in Nonsense are chosen according to the contribution they can make in this respect.

Emphasis on a careful choice, and a suggestion of the principle by which that choice is made, occur in Lear's self-portrait in verse, 'How pleasant to know Mr. Lear!' from which the title of this chapter is taken. The particular verse runs as follows:—

His mind is concrete and fastidious,
His nose is remarkably big;

His visage is more or less hideous,
His beard it resembles a wig.

It sounds like a bad pun to say that this should be taken
at its face value; but the last three lines are true, as Lear
would have been the first to admit, and there is no reason
to doubt the veracity of the first one. Throughout Nonsense there is, as we shall see, a recurrent pattern suggesting
a rigour in selection which might well be termed fastidiousness, and a careful addiction to the concrete or, rather,
to words which refer to concrete things.

Fastidiousness and concreteness in a mind imply rejection of a great deal as unsuitable to the purpose in hand,
and a turning towards the normal and familiar things
of experience which after all are the basis of our notion
of 'one and one and one' in real life. So Saint Thomas
says, 'The principle of singularity is matter' (*Summa*, Pt. I,
Q. 14, Art. 11). Both of these processes, the enclosure and
restriction of the field and the turning from the immaterial
to the material, fit very well with the principles of a game as
we have so far discovered them. A game must have objects
to play with, and must be conducted in a restricted area.

We had better take a restricted area ourselves at this
point if we are going to see how these principles work out
in Nonsense, and we might do worse than concentrate for
the present on the verses which occur in the two Alices.
It has already been suggested that these may be closer to
the almost wholly versified world of Lear and Nursery
Rhyme than Carroll's prose. They have a further advantage in that seven of the sixteen sets of verses occurring in
these works are parodies, and the process of parody may
provide helpful evidence, because it shows the exact nature
of the author's choice and of his rejections. There follows
a list of the verses:—

ALICE'S ADVENTURES IN WONDERLAND

1. How doth the little crocodile . . . From 'How doth the
   little busy bee' by Isaac Watts.

2. Fury said to a mouse.
3. You are old, Father William . . . From *The Old Man's Comforts and how he gained them* by Southey.
4. Speak roughly to your little boy.
5. Twinkle, twinkle, little bat . . . From 'Twinkle, twinkle, little star' by Jane Taylor.
6. Will you walk a little faster.
7. 'Tis the voice of the lobster. . . . From ''Tis the voice of the sluggard' by Watts.
8. Beautiful Soup.
9. They told me you had been to her.

THROUGH THE LOOKING-GLASS

1. Jabberwocky.
2. The Walrus and the Carpenter.
3. In winter, when the fields are white.
4. I'll tell thee everything I can . . . From *Resolution and Independence* by Wordsworth.
5. Hush a by lady on Alice's lap. . . . From 'Rockaby baby on the treetop.'
6. To the Looking-Glass World
   it was Alice that said. . . . From *Bonnie Dundee*.
7. First the fish must be caught.

In our four groups of words mentioned earlier we had the rough headings: number words, thing words, abstracts and gibberish. In the Carroll verses number and thing words occur together in 'To the Looking-Glass world',

> Put cats in the coffee and mice in the tea,
> And welcome Queen Alice with thirty-times-three!

and in the White Knight's song,

> And these I do not sell for gold
> Or coin of silvery shine,
> But for a copper halfpenny,
> And that will purchase nine.

Things are the basis of 'How doth the little crocodile', 'Twinkle, twinkle' and *The Walrus and the Carpenter*. What happens to abstracts will be seen in Father William and

"'Tis the voice of the lobster'. Jabberwocky will provide an example of the fourth group, of Nonsense verbiage. In addition, we have two problems in what one might call un-attached relations, in Humpty Dumpty's song,

> The little fishes answer was
> 'We cannot do it, Sir, because——'

and in the verses read at the trial of the Knave of Hearts,

> I gave her one, they gave him two,
> You gave us three or more;
> They all returned from him to you,
> Though they were mine before.

and there is a riddling pun, without any answer given, in the last Looking-Glass song, 'First the fish must be caught'. We will start with the first two groups, number and thing words, and see how the rest fits in later.

Chapter 7

CATS, COFFEE, AND
THIRTY-TIMES-THREE

THE SERIES of whole numbers, 0, 1, 2, 3 and so on, is a simple series proceeding without repetition to infinity. With the exception of the first term, each term in the series can in theory be reached by adding one to the preceding term, so that whenever a number occurs, 92, let us say, the mind knows that this represents a particular point in the number series. Any plurality occurring in experience can in theory be found to correspond with some point on the number scale. This is where the notion of correspondence between classes comes in, a basic notion in the definition of number itself.

There seem to be three things implicit in any mental act involving a number. First, each whole number is regarded as separate and distinct from any other, i.e. 9 is not 10. Second, any given number implies for the mind the familiar series of all the numbers; we know that 92 comes between 91 and 93, and that the numbers run back from 92 to 0 and onwards from 92 till we get tired of counting. Third, any given number sets a limit, because it represents a particular point in the series. These three accompaniments of the notion of number—distinctness of the units, establishment of a series, limitation—link up with the conditions for play suggested in Chapter 4.

The first of these three, the separateness of the integers as such, need not concern us very much. It is an unquestioned convention of number working, but we are not enquiring into the nature of numbers as such. These are the affair of the arithmetician and do not enter much into writing or Nonsense. They occur in one place in *Through the Looking-Glass*, in the Humpty Dumpty chapter:—

'How many days are there in a year?'

'Three hundred and sixty-five,' said Alice.

'And how many birthdays have you?'

'One.'

'And if you take one from three hundred and sixty-five what remains?'

'Three hundred and sixty-four, of course.'

Humpty Dumpty looked doubtful. 'I'd rather see that done on paper,' he said.

Alice couldn't help smiling as she took out her memorandum book, and worked the sum for him:

$$365$$
$$1$$
$$\overline{}$$
$$364$$
$$\overline{}$$

Humpty Dumpty took the book and looked at it carefully. 'That seems to be done right——' he began.

Humpty Dumpty requires the figuring of the sum as well as its expression in words, so that he may the better verify the arithmetic; Alice is scornful of this proceeding, but it is sound enough, and interesting from our point of view for it suggests that it is important to Nonsense that numbers and arithmetic should work properly. There are two other sums in Carroll's Nonsense, one in the Snark:—

'Taking Three as the subject to reason about—
    A convenient number to state—
We add Seven, and Ten, and then multiply out
    By One Thousand diminished by Eight.

'The result we proceed to divide, as you see,
    By Nine Hundred and Ninety and Two:
Then subtract Seventeen, and the answer must be
    Exactly and perfectly true.'

The other is in *Through the Looking-Glass*, when Alice is musing over the first chorus of the song at her banquet:—

Then followed a confused noise of cheering, and Alice

thought to herself, 'Thirty times three makes ninety. I wonder if anyone's counting.'

This is in a sense Nonsense arithmetic, and although Nonsense is not concerned with arithmetic as such, it is noticeable that this figuring is valid. There is no playing about with the nature of number, no suggestion that in Nonsense three and two make six. Numbers are accepted here just as they are in ordinary life, as infallible. Sums are right or wrong. This is interesting in view of the theory that Nonsense is dream literature, for numbers in dreams behave very oddly indeed. Freud says in *The Interpretation of Dreams* that the dreamer cannot do arithmetic.[1] St. Thomas maintains that syllogisms go wrong in dreams (*Summa*, Pt. I, Q. 84, Art. 8). The absolute reliability of the arithmetic in Carroll's Nonsense does not suggest the dreaming mind.

There is one thing about numbers which concerns Nonsense very closely, however, and that is the fact that they have names as well as ciphers, and so belong also in the world of language. The particular usefulness of numbers to the mind depends on this, since they form a convenient series of mental concepts which can be used to order the facts of experience, and which can be translated into the mind's normal means of communication, words. By means of numbers the mind can endow experience with the characteristics of a series—order, limitation, division into separate units. In this way the conditions for a game are set up, and the mind can play and juggle with its notions of experience as it could never do without the help of numbers. These are also the conditions for scientific thinking, which as time goes on becomes more and more numerical and mathematical. But in ordinary thinking, too, we require that there shall be a correspondence between the universe of things and the universe of numbers, not merely in high and lofty matters but in quite ordinary ones, with which we, like Nonsense writers, are much more con-

[1] George Allen & Unwin Ltd., London, 1913, pp. 325–9.

cerned. The fact that number is expressible in words forms the main bridge between the abstract concept of number—which could live its own life perfectly well without words at all in the realm of figures and symbols—and the things of this world.

Number words, as *words*, form part of the material of Nonsense. We saw in the last chapter that they have certain peculiarities, shared only with technical terms: simple and precise reference, and no variability. They are limited and exact, and so possess characteristics of order and predictability which are absent from most of language and most of life. For this reason they are ideal play material for Nonsense. But Nonsense does not play with them on their own. Its aim, as we have seen, is to draw language on to the side of order in the mind, and so it must attempt to organize, with the help of words, and number, and number-words, the complex muddle which goes by the name of 'experience' in any mind. This is in no way to go against the grain of the mind's working. The mind enjoys order, and employs language, in prose, to fulfil this very function. Nonsense tries to take the process one stage further.

In the ordinary use of language the qualities of number and order which we have been talking about in this chapter, distinctness of units, maintenance of an ordered series, exact definition, are only very imperfectly attained. This is no accident, for life itself is only partially orderly as far as the mind can tell, and so language by being a mixture of order and disorder fulfils its purpose of being coextensive and united with experience in the mind and of rendering that experience communicable. We are content to manage certain bits of life, and to have certain bits manage us; indeed we have no choice in the matter. The same thing is true of language. We accept the fact that certain bits of it are under our control and certain bits not. If, however, as is the case with Nonsense, words are used as playthings, then this half-and-half state of affairs will not do. Our material will have to be under our control, because in a game the player must not be played with, as our minds are played with, in part at least, by the words which we see and hear and use and imagine we are controlling. The material is the same, words and a mind's images of experience as crystallized in words, but the product will have to be rather different from ordinary life in some way. Nonsense does indeed differ from ordinary experience:—

> But they said, 'If you choose, To boil eggs in your shoes . . .'
>
> (LEAR, M.N.)
>
> A large blue caterpillar . . . quietly smoking a long hookah.
>
> (*The Rabbit Sends in a Little Bill*, A.A.W.)
>
> Upon Paul's steeple stands a tree
> As full of apples as can be . . .

But it begins to look as if this is due not to a decrease in order but to an increase, an attempt to make the mind create for itself a more orderly universe; and inevitably this will pull normal life a little out of shape.

The Nonsense writer wants to make a world out of language and the mind's pattern of reality, but reality which will be remade so as to be more subject to number; and the characteristics of number and order will have to be imparted to the images in the mind so that they too may be controlled, distinguishable from one another, going along one at a time in an ordered series, limited and exact. If this can be accomplished, the mind's perceptions of the normal things of life, trees and birds and animals and clothes and food and so on, will be brought under stricter control than is usual in language, and in this state they could be played with. Numbers and the facts of perception seem in themselves reliable and certain to the mind, and with this added control they will seem more so. That is all to the good, for it is essential to the working of a game that the mind should feel safe inside it. It is this sense of safety which the game's rules and limitations are intended to ensure, making a game more certain than life can be. St. Thomas makes a similar distinction between life and art, saying, 'Thus matters of art, though they are singular, are never-the-less more fixed and certain, wherefore in many of them there is no room for counsel on account of their certitude' (*Summa*, Pt. II—II, Q. 49, Art. 5). The certitude is achieved in each case in the same way—by limitation through fixed rules.

As the starting-point of the game of Nonsense, we have the two systems, number and the mind's experience of reality, united by the fact that they are both expressible in language. The first is wholly abstract, while the second consists of impressions derived from actual phenomena, the mind's realization of the fact that 'the world is so full of a number of things'. Nonsense can deal with this material in one of two ways. It can either employ the number series and a series of things separately, establishing the serial character of each but letting them just run parallel, without direct meeting; or it can let them meet and join. This distinction will become clearer in a moment. The first method establishes two series, one of number units, the other of thing units, side by side. The second relies on pinning down a particular collection of things by correlating it with a point on the number scale, thus making it exact and limited. Phenomena in real life can be thought of as units or collections; number, by virtue of its serial character and its limiting precision, can manage both, or perhaps one should say, can give the mind the impression that it is managing both.

We can follow up the suggestion in the last chapter, and take one of Carroll's sets of verses as an example of the first manœuvre.

> Then fill up the glasses as quick as you can,
> And sprinkle the table with buttons and bran:
> Put cats in the coffee and mice in the tea—
> And welcome Queen Alice with thirty-times-three!

This is the first chorus of the Looking-Glass creatures' song at Alice's feast, and the second follows the same lines:—

> Then fill up the glasses with treacle and ink,
> Or anything else that is pleasant to drink:
> Mix sand with the cider and wool with the wine—
> And welcome Queen Alice with ninety-times-nine!

There is no logical connection between the buttons, bran, cats, coffee, mice and tea of the first verse, the treacle, ink, sand, cider, wool and wine of the second, and the numbers introduced, 30×3 and 90×9. Two separate series are touched off in the mind. The second, the series of whole numbers, is not in any way related, by reference, to the first which is a series of things; but, as the mention of any number must do, it sets the mind running along the familiar and ordered series of natural numbers. The mind by the very mention of number is delivered into the hands of its own ordering tendency. This may seem odd, because the other series in the above examples, cats and coffee and so on, the explicit series of thing-words as opposed to the series implicit in the mention of number, is apparently highly disordered. This is not chance, however, and there is no inconsistency. The point is that when once the number series is established, the reader will be in a serial frame of mind, fortified by the strictly numerical rhythms of the verse itself; and the incongruity of the thing series will not matter. On the contrary, it is an essential part of the process, for a series has to consist of separate and distinct terms, units going along one and one and one, and therefore the incompatibility of the things listed is a help rather than a hindrance to the ordering force in the mind. Just because they are so separate from one another it can the more readily arrange them one and one and one. If the things mentioned were not incompatible, or were less so, the mind would start trying to put them together and to fuse them into a whole, which would lead not to Nonsense but to poetry. The number series would then perform its usual function in poetry, nourishing and holding steady the force towards order in the mind while allowing the force towards disorder full play in the system of reference. Here is an example of this very thing:—

> I'll sing you twelve—o!
> *Green grow the rushes—o!*
> What is your twelve—o?
>> Twelve for the twelve Apostles,
>> Eleven for the eleven who went to Heaven
>> And ten for the Ten Commandments,
>> Nine for the nine bright shiners
>> And eight for the April rainers,
>> Seven for the seven stars in the sky
>> And six for the six proud walkers,
>> Five for the symbol at your door
>> And four for the Gospel-makers,
>> Three, three the rivals,
>> Two, two the lily-white boys,
>>> clothed all in green-o,
>> And one is one and all alone
>>> and evermore shall be so.

Here the number series is established explicitly; but the uncertain meaning of some of the terms used in the other series, the thing series, allows the dream and disorder faculty of the mind to run them together, and removes the whole out of the field of Nonsense, not into sense but into poetry. The same thing happens with the higher numbers in *The Twelve Days of Christmas*:—

> On the twelfth day of Christmas my true love gave to me
>> Twelve lords a-leaping,
>> Eleven ladies dancing,
>> Ten pipers piping,
>> Nine drummers drumming,
>> Eight maids a-milking,
>> Seven swans a-swimming,
>> Six geese a-laying,
>>> Five gold rings,
>> Four colley birds,
>> Three French hens,
>> Two turtle doves, and
> A partridge in a pear tree.

Here, as far as the five gold rings, we are in the world of poetry, but after that Nonsense starts to come in, introduced by the colley birds, whatever they may be, and we end in Nonsense proper because partridges and pear trees will not fuse completely in the mind, and a sense of incongruity allows the mind to slip back into its double series, the two running parallel, numbers here, things there.

Anything can go into the thing series provided that the list when drawn up will defeat the dream tendency of the mind to run things together. That dream tendency is always there, so that the achievement of the necessary degree of incongruity is a definite part of the game. It is in this way that the mind is given freedom, and the process explains why Nonsense is not lunacy and is not frightening. The use of number as the basic type of ordered series lends the mind a fixed and reliable serial framework, a row of boxes into which the mind is then free to pop all kinds of surprising things. Nonsense makes full use of this:—

> One, two,
> Buckle my shoe.
> Three, four,
> Open the door.
> Five, six,
> Pick up sticks.
> Seven, eight,
> Lay them straight . . .

> One, two, three, four,
> Mother caught a jackdaw,
> Put it out the back door,
> One, two, three, four.

> One, two, three, four, five,
> Once I caught a fish alive.
> Why did you let it go?
> Because it bit my fingers so.
> Which finger did it bite?
> The little finger on the right.

This old man, he played one,
He played nick nack on my gun.
Nick nack paddywack, give a dog a bone,
This old man came rolling home.

This old man, he played two,
He played nick nack on my shoe.

This old man, he played three,
He played nick nack on my knee.

This old man, he played four,
He played nick nack on my door . . .

The animals went in two by two,
    There's one more river to cross.
The elephant and the kangaroo,
    One more river to cross.
        One more river,
        And that's the river of Jordan,
        One more river,
    There's one more river to cross.

The animals went in three by three . . .
The rhinoceros arm in arm with the flea . . .

Go to bed first, a golden purse.
Go to bed second, a golden pheasant.
Go to bed third, a golden bird.

In all these examples, as in the one from the Looking-Glass, what one might call the meaning of number, the reference-content of nine or ten or eleven, has no connection with the things mentioned. There is no rational link between the cats and the coffee and thirty-times-three, and this does not matter at all; nor does it matter that Alice cannot do the sum of ninety-times-nine at the end of the second verse, because in one sense the sum has no answer. The purpose of the numbers is merely to give the mind that sense of security and of being in control of the situation which comes from the contemplation of an ordered series. It is the form of the number series, not the content, which serves the purpose of Nonsense in cases like these.

This leads on to another point, for although number is the most familiar example of a series of this kind, the mental prototype of THE SERIES, it is not the only one, and Nonsense makes use of any others that may come to hand as substitutes for the number series or in addition to it, provided only that they are familiar to the mind. Nonsense is less fussy than mathematics here, for the latter requires that any progression from which an arithmetic is to be constructed should be infinite; but Nonsense will be content with very much less. In fact, it can manage with that smallest of all series, the series with only two terms. The following are examples of such series at work. The first two are very small series of names from Scripture:—

> Said Aaron to Moses,
> 'Let's cut off our noses.'
> Said Moses to Aaron,
> ''Tis the fashion to wear 'em.'

> Shadrach
> Shake the bed;
> Meshech
> Make the bed;
> And Abednego,
> And to bed we go.

The beginnings of a Latin conjugation will do:—

> *Amo, amas,*
> I love a lass . . .

So will three positions in time, as in the 'Go to bed first' rhyme already quoted; or three positions in space:—

> He that lies at the stock
> Shall have the gold rock.
> He that lies at the wall
> Shall have the gold ball.
> He that lies in the middle
> Shall have the gold fiddle.

So will a list of the City Churches of London:—

> 'Oranges and lemons'
> Say the bells of Saint Clement's.

F

'You owe me five farthings'
Say the bells of Saint Martin's.

'Kettles and pans'
Say the bells of Saint Anne's.

'Two sticks and an apple'
Say the bells of Whitechapel.

'Brickbats and tiles'
Say the bells of Saint Giles.

The days of the week make another such series:—

Solomon Grundy,
Born on Monday,
Christened on Tuesday,
Married on Wednesday,
Took ill on Thursday,
Worse on Friday,
Died on Saturday,
Buried on Sunday,
This was the end of Solomon Grundy.

So do the five fingers or toes:—

This little pig went to market,
This little pig stayed at home,
This little pig had roast beef,
This little pig had none,
And this little pig went Wee Wee Wee Wee all
the way home.

So does a sequence of cause and effect:—

This was the maiden all forlorn
That milked the cow with the crumpled horn
That tossed the dog
That worried the cat
That killed the rat
That ate the malt
That lay in the house that Jack built.

The manœuvre can be executed particularly well with
the letters of the alphabet, a comparatively long series and
as familiar to the mind as numbers themselves.

A, B, C,
Tumbledown D,
The cat's in the cupboard
And can't see me.

Great A, little a,
Bouncing B . . .

A was an Apple-pie.
A ate it.
B bit it.
C cut it.
D dealt it . . .

Lear makes much use of this, having to his credit no less than six Nonsense alphabets. Given below, to show the type of treatment, is what he produced for the letter M in each of these.

M was a mill
Which stood on a hill
And turned round and round
With a loud hummy sound.
   m!
   useful old mill!

M was once a little mouse,
  Mousey
  Bousey
  Sousy
  Mousy
In the housy,
Little Mouse.

M was a man,
Who walked round and round,
And he wore a long coat
That came down to the ground.
   m!
   Funny old Man!

The Melodious Meritorious Mouse,
who played a merry minuet on the Piano-forte.

M was a dish of Mince;
It looked so good to eat!
Papa, he quickly ate it up,
And said, 'This is a treat!'

M said, 'A Mulberry or two might give him
satisfaction.'

Lear also uses a small series of letters as a chorus in the
Discobbolos verses:—

'From worry of life we've fled—
Oh! W! X! Y! Z!
There is no more trouble ahead,
Sorrow or any such thing—
For Mr. and Mrs. Discobbolos!'
(L.L.)

Carroll does not use the alphabet series as such, but it is
perhaps worth noticing his fondness for writing verse acrostics on names, such as 'A boat, beneath a sunny sky', the
initial letters of whose lines spell the name of the original
Alice, ALICE PLEASANCE LIDDELL.

So far we have been dealing with explicit series, but
behind these lie what one might call shadow series, implied
but not expressed. This brings us to what in poetry is
called, significantly enough, enumeration, and to rhyme,
rhythm and repetition. Number as such, in its form of 1, 2,
3, 4, seems to have vanished here, but the notion of a
series, of things going along one and one and one, is still
there.

Enumeration or lists of things form an essential part
of Nonsense. We may have a list of names:—

With Bill Brewer, Jan Stewer, Peter Gurney, Peter Davy,
Dan'l Whiddon, 'Arry 'Awke, old Uncle Tom Cobbley and all.

It may take the form of an oddly assorted collection, as in
the two following examples, which come somewhere between Nonsense and poetry because the ingredients are
not quite incompatible enough to be true Nonsense:—

Sing levy dew, sing levy dew,
    The water and the wine,
The seven bright gold wires
    And the bugles that do shine.

With, lily, germander and sops-in-wine,
    With sweetbriar
    And bonfire
    And strawberry wire
And columbine.

There is a wonderful list in T. H. White's *The Sword in the Stone*, describing the contents of Merlyn's room and going on almost unbroken for a page and a half:—

> . . . an astrolabe, twelve pairs of boots, a dozen purse-nets, three dozen rabbit wires, twelve corkscrews, an ant's nest between two glass plates, ink-bottles of every possible colour from red to violet, darning-needles, a gold medal for being the best scholar at Eton, four or five recorders, a nest of field mice all alive-o, two skulls, plenty of cut glass. . . .

There are some good examples in Lear's letters:—

> I am quite crazy about Memphis and On and Isis and crocodiles and ophthalmia and nubians and simooms and sorcerers and sphingidoe.
>
>   (Letter to Chichester Fortescue, October 9th, 1856)
>
> I meant to have written a lot about the priests and the signori, and the good peasantry, and the orange-trees, and the sea-gulls, and geraniums, and the Ionian Ball, and Jerusalem Artichokes, and Colonel Paterson, and old Dandolo's palm-tree, and my spectacles, and the East-wind, and Zambelli's nasty little dogs, and fishermen, and Scarpe's cats, and whatnot, but I am too sleepy.
>
>   (January 18th, 1858)
>
> Write upon prawns, rheumatism, Armstrong guns, Birds of Paradise or raspberry jam—so you write.
>
>   (October 3rd, 1862)

As Gilbert says in a rather different connection, it doesn't really matter whom you put upon the list, and Lear and

Carroll make good use of this. The list of things the White Knight is said to have on his horse's back is an example—a bee-hive, a mouse-trap, a bag with candlesticks in it, bunches of carrots, fire-irons. Here is one from Lear:—

> And they bought an Owl, and a useful Cart,
> And a pound of Rice, and a Cranberry Tart,
> And a hive of silvery Bees.
> And they bought a Pig, and some green Jack-daws,
> And a lovely Monkey with lollipop paws,
> And forty bottles of Ring-Bo-Ree,
> And no end of Stilton Cheese.
>
> (*The Jumblies*, N.S.B.)

If lists have been a recognized Nonsense procedure from Rabelais onwards, so, too, have rhyme, rhythm and repetition. Cammaerts (*op. cit.* p. 39 ff.) says of the Nonsense writer, 'He uses a perfect orgy of refrains and repetitions . . . Commentators are often puzzled by the strangeness of some nursery rhyme's refrain which has no relation whatever with the story'; and he adds, 'It is not for us to solve the riddle of the refrain.' In this implicit notion of a series which they bring with them, however, may lie the key to their use, both in poetry and Nonsense. The crucial point is this: that a recurrence, whether of a sound as in rhyme, a particular letter or group of letters as in alliteration, or a group of words as in a refrain, is still a series. If we were speaking loosely, we might say that each instance is identical with every other; but that is just what it is not. Strictly speaking there is no question of identity between one occurrence of a refrain and the next. They seem precisely similar, but the mind says, 'Here it comes again, for the third time', or 'Here it is again, a bit farther down the page.' The implicit notion of a series is there, indeed this type of series is the exact equivalent of 'one and one and one and one' which we were talking about earlier. This serial quality in repetition is not an invention of my own; it is accepted mathematically in the form of a pseudo-series, in which repetitions of certain terms occur, which can be correlated with a true series in which there are no repetitions.[1]

Refrain, alliteration and rhyme are all going to come under the category of pseudo-series which suggest to the mind the true, unrepeating series behind them. The use of the refrain in Lear and Carroll is so common that it need not be dwelt on. With Carroll it may be as simple as the 'Wow! wow! wow!' of the Pepper Song in the Duchess's Kitchen, or may appear as, 'Will you, won't you, will you, won't you, won't you join the dance?' or 'Beautiful, beautiful Soup!' Lear gives a chorus to the Jumblies narrative, 'Far and few, far and few . . .' to the Pelicans, 'Ploffskin, Pluffskin, Pelican jee!', to the Discobbolos songs, to *Calico Pie*. The refrain is used over and over again in rhymes and ballads:—

> *With a roly-poly, gammon and spinach,*
> *Heigh-ho, says Anthony Rowley.*

> London Bridge is broken down,
> *Dance over, my lady lee,*
> London Bridge is broken down,
> *With a gay lady.*

> Here comes a lusty wooer,
> *My a dildin, my a daldin,*
> Here comes a lusty wooer,
> *Lily bright and shine-a.*

These are cases where the repetition is created and introduced by the writer himself to serve as a series; but the chances of language also provide series of repetitions, and the Nonsense writer makes use of these, in the form of alliteration and rhyme. As with the other series we have been considering, these may be very small:—

> Little birds are bathing
> Crocodiles in cream . . .

[1] Cf. Whitehead and Russell, *Principia Mathematica*, Cambridge University Press, 1910, Vol. II, Pt. V, pp. 513–14.

Little birds are choking
  Baronets with bun . . .
                              (*The Pig-Tale*, s.b.c.)

Sing Beans, sing Bones, sing Butterflies!

.   .   .   .   .   .

Sing Prunes, sing Prawns, sing Primrose-Hill!

.   .   .   .   .   .

Sing Flies, sing Frogs, sing Fiddle-Strings!

.   . .   .

Sing Cats, sing Corks, sing Cowslip-Tea!
                              (*Bruno's Lessons*, s.b.c.)

'What does it live on?' Alice asked, with great curiosity.
'Sap and sawdust,' said the Gnat.
                              (*Looking-Glass Insects*, t.l.g.)

'They were learning to draw,' the Dormouse went on,
yawning and rubbing its eyes, for it was getting very
sleepy; 'and they drew all manner of things—everything
that begins with an M——'
'Why with an M?' said Alice.
'Why not?' said the March Hare.
Alice was silent.
The Dormouse had closed its eyes by this time, and was
going off into a doze; but, on being pinched by the Hatter,
it woke up again with a little shriek, and went on: '—that
begins with an M, such as mouse-traps, and the moon, and
memory, and muchness. . . .'
                              (*A Mad Tea-Party*, a.a.w.)

Lear produces the same kind of thing:—

the Tropical Turnspits which frequented the neighbour-
hood . . .
                              (*The Four Little Children*, n.s.b.)

they saw on the 15th day of their travels, a bright blue
Boss-woss . . .
                              (*The Seven Families*, n.s.b.)

The Inventive Indian,
who caught a Remarkable Rabbit in a
Stupendous Silver Spoon.

The Visibly Vicious Vulture,
who wrote some verses to a Veal-cutlet in a
Volume bound in Vellum.

(M.N.)

These muttering, miserable, mutton-hating, man-avoid-
ing, misogynic, morose and merriment-marring, mono-
toning, many-mule-making, mocking, mournful, minced-
fish and marmalade-masticating Monx.

(Letter on the monks of Mount Athos, to
Chichester Fortescue, January 3rd, 1858)

In the same way, words that by the chances of language
development have the same sound provide the Nonsense
writer with another source of series. We can take as our
example the following series of words which are brought
together by the fact of rhyme: big, pig, wig, fig, gig, jig.
Nursery Rhyme starts them off:—

As I was going to Bonner
  I met a pig
  Without a wig,
Upon my word and honour.

Barber, barber, shave a pig;
How many hairs to make a wig?

To market, to market to buy a fat pig,
Home again, home again, jiggety-jig!

Lear has a wonderful time with this set of words:—

There was a Young Lady of Bute,
Who played on a silver-gilt flute;
She played several jigs, to her uncle's white pigs,
That amusing Young Lady of Bute.

(B.N.)

They called aloud, 'Our Sieve ain't big,
But we don't care a button! we don't care a fig!
In a Sieve we'll go to sea!'

(*The Jumblies*, N.S.B.)

There was an old man of Messina,
Whose daughter was named Opsibeena;
She wore a small wig, and rode out on a pig,
To the perfect delight of Messina.

(N.S.B.)

There was an old person of Bray,
Who sang through the whole of the day
To his ducks and his pigs, whom he fed upon figs,
That valuable person of Bray.

(N.S.B.)

There was an old person of Ealing,
Who was wholly devoid of good feeling;
He drove a small gig, with three Owls and a Pig,
Which distressed all the people of Ealing.

(N.S.B.)

It occurs in Carroll too:—

'Did you say "pig" or "fig"?' said the Cat.
'I said "pig",' replied Alice.

(*Pig and Pepper*, A.A.W.)

The reader will have noticed, from these and earlier examples, that none of these series is exclusive. The writer is free to employ as many of them simultaneously as he can handle, provided only, so far as Nonsense is concerned, that the serial order in the mind is maintained, and that the mind is kept in the world of number and not allowed to stray into the world of dream where the elements may start to fuse into poetry. So far we have looked at the first two properties of Number which we set out to investigate in this chapter, namely, distinctness of units and the establishment of a series. We now come to the third, limitation, for this is the point at which number and things, which so far have been running along more or less parallel, are going to meet.

Chapter 8

SEVEN MAIDS WITH
SEVEN MOPS

WE HAVE seen how Nonsense employs series (particularly the basic series of natural numbers), sometimes simply, sometimes two or three at a time, allowing different series to run along side by side but always preserving the conditions necessary for serial order, the integrity of the units and an arrangement turning upon some form of 'before' and 'after'. This process works well on the whole, but it has to be watched because there is, for the game of Nonsense, a danger inherent in certain types of series. Some of the series used are, as we have seen, small and limited in their nature. You cannot squeeze an indefinite number of people into one bed, for instance, nor can there be an infinite number of churches in London. Series are not necessarily limited in this way, however, and the basic series, number, is infinite. Now any game—and Nonsense is no exception—must be carefully limited. It can have no truck with infinity; but equally if it chooses to play with number it cannot alter the nature of the number concept and remove infinity from it.

This is not all. The examples given showed that for the number series could be substituted series of things, phenomena of one kind or another forming part of experience. In the Nonsense game, care is taken to make these phenomena into singulars and individuals by insisting on their incongruity. Here again, however, the same danger appears. 'Singulars are infinite', as St. Thomas says (*Summa*, Pt. I—II, Q. 14, Art. 6); he adds that they are so 'not actually but only potentially', but even this potential infinity threatens to upset Nonsense just as much as the potential infinity of the numbers series, and the danger is all the greater because number and things are in this game the principal playthings. Nonsense is a construction of the reason; but if it is true that 'it belongs to the reason to proceed to infinity' (*Summa*, Pt. I—II, Q. 30, Art 4), Nonsense is in a quandary. It has to keep its world small, limited and controlled if it is to manipulate it, and manipulation is an essential feature of play. The problem occurs in other spheres besides Nonsense; Whitehead, for instance, in a particularly interesting passage in *Essays in Science and Philosophy*, pp. 103–6, says that even in arithmetic you cannot get rid of a sub-conscious reference to the unbounded universe, speaks of the futility, the superstitious awe, of infinitude, and adds, 'All value is the gift of finitude which is the necessary condition for activity,' and ends by saying that eventually all forms of thought will have to go back to Symbolic Logic, which will bring them full circle back to St. Thomas Aquinas.

The act of assigning a number to a particular collection occurring in experience consists in establishing a correlation between it and its appropriate class on the number scale. In theory this is always possible with any collection experience may produce, and when a number has been assigned, the collection is limited as far as the mind is concerned by this precise correspondence between class and class. In Nonsense it need not matter that no examples of either class actually exist, provided that the mind sees the possibility of correlating one with another, as for instance in the rhyme,

> The man in the wilderness said to me,
> 'How many strawberries grow in the sea?'
> I answered him as I thought good,
> 'As many as red herrings grow in the wood.'

Giving a collection the name of a number makes it definite and almost turns it into an individual. But at the outset there is a difficulty which affects Nonsense or any other form of activity which requires limitation, since there are certain multiplicities in the world which cannot in practice be numbered. Where this happens, the writer can do one of two things. Either he can admit the impossibility of using number as a scale by which to assess this particular collection, and the result will be this type of thing:—

> After this I beheld, and, lo, a great multitude, which no man could number, of all nations, and kindreds, and people, and tongues, stood before the throne, and before the Lamb.
>
> (REVELATIONS vii. 9)

or, in a very different context, this:—

> Sleep on, ye pale civilians,
>   All thunder-clouds defy:
> On Europe's countless millions
> The Sentry keeps his eye!
>
> (W. S. GILBERT, *Iolanthe*)

Or he can abandon number as the scale against which measurements are to be made, and employ instead another of the unnumbered multitudes of the world of things, measuring one infinity against another, as in the following:—

> The Lord your God hath multiplied you, and behold, ye are this day as the stars of heaven for multitude.
>
> (DEUTERONOMY i. 10)

> For innumerable evils have compassed me about: mine iniquities have taken hold upon me so that I am not able to look up; they are more than the hairs of mine head: therefore my heart faileth me.
>
> (PSALM xl. 12)

> The atoms of Democritus
> And Newton's particles of light
> Are sands upon the Red Sea shore
> Where Israel's tents do shine so bright.
>
> (BLAKE)

Sometimes two of these are employed together for added emphasis:—

> . . . That in blessing I will bless thee, and in multiplying

I will multiply thy seed as the stars of heaven, and as the
sand which is upon the sea shore.

(GENESIS xxii. 17)

Here are three sample types of an uncountable infinity of
things, the hairs of the head, the stars, and the sand on the
shore. It is interesting that the numbering of these is
reserved explicitly to God alone, the Infinite controlling
infinitude and perhaps therefore playing with it.

The number of drops of rain and the sand of the sea are
certain to God.

(*Summa*, Pt. I, Q 23, Art. 7)

But the very hairs of your head are all numbered.

(ST. MATTHEW, x. 30)

He telleth the number of the stars; he calleth them all by
their names.

(PSALM cxlvii. 4)

That last example goes one better, suggesting that God
has a dual notation, numbers and words, for that particular
multitude. And the stars and the sand of the sea shore
bring us directly—and I mean no irreverence—to *The
Walrus and the Carpenter*.

The poem opens with a description, three verses long,
of a night scene. The sun is up in the sky, along with the
moon, and, as the verses admit,

> . . . this was odd, because it was
> The middle of the night.

We accept this, however, since the writer is free to build
his own universe, and we wait to see what it will be like.
But if both sun and moon are present, there are no stars.
One multitude, one standard type of infinity, has been
suppressed. Is this accidental? I do not want to press the
point. Instead, we can move on to the fourth verse:—

> The Walrus and the Carpenter
> Were walking close at hand;
> They wept like anything to see

> Such quantities of sand:
> 'If this were only cleared away,'
>   They said, 'it *would* be grand!'

Here is another ancient type of infinity, the grains of sand; of course they want it out of the way, and the method proposed for getting rid of it is interesting.

> 'If seven maids with seven mops
>   Swept it for half a year,
> Do you suppose,' the Walrus said,
>   'That they could get it clear?'
> 'I doubt it,' said the Carpenter,
>   And shed a bitter tear.

There are three numbers here in two lines of verse, seven agents, seven instruments, and six months. Even so, they are admitted to be inadequate, since the mind cannot conquer the innumerable with numbers; and so there is weeping at the end, and a change of subject to something that can be numbered and kept properly under control.

> 'O Oysters, come and walk with us!'
>   The Walrus did beseech,
> 'A pleasant walk, a pleasant talk,
>   Along the briny beach:
> We cannot do with more than four,
>   To give a hand to each.'

It is pleasing that Nonsense also produces a rather similar attempt to deal with the infinity of the hairs of the head, in the rhyme already quoted in another connection:—

> Barber, barber, shave a pig.
> How many hairs to make a wig?

The answer is very like that of the Walrus and Carpenter, since it also employs number, completely inadequately,

> Four and twenty, that's enough!

and then there follows what looks like a deliberate attempt to distract somebody's attention:

> Give the barber a pinch of snuff!

In these examples the rule holds good that the Carroll characters seem to be commenting on the game while it is going on, whereas the Nursery Rhyme ones are just playing it. The same thing happens with those other apparent infinities which play a part in experience, Space and Time. As infinities, they are unsuitable for Nonsense to play with, or to play in. The limiting process, which is achieved by dividing the apparent given continuum into numbered intervals on which the mind can concentrate, so forgetting the infinity, is a constant feature of Nonsense:—

> There was an old woman went up in a basket,
> Seventy times as high as the moon.

> How many miles to Babylon?
> Three score miles and ten.

There are dozens of examples in Lear:—

> There was a Young Girl of Majorca,
> Whose aunt was a very fast walker;
> She walked seventy miles, and leaped fifteen stiles,
> Which astonished that Girl of Majorca.
> (B.N.)

> For his hat was a hundred and two feet wide,
> With ribbons and bibbons on every side
> (The Quangle Wangle's Hat, L.L.)

> It was perfectly beautiful, and contained only a single tree, 503 feet high.
> (The Four Little Children, N.S.B.)

> And if you ever happen to go to Gramble-Blamble, and visit that museum in the city of Tosh, look for them on the Ninety-eighth table in the Four hundred and twenty-seventh room of the right-hand corridor of the left wing of the Central Quadrangle of that magnificent building; for if you do not, you certainly will not see them.
> (The Seven Families, N.S.B.)

Carroll not only provides examples of this kind of thing, he points out the necessity for precision and measurement:—

'While you're refreshing yourself,' said the Queen, 'I'll just take the measurements.' And she took a ribbon out of her pocket marked in inches, and began measuring the ground, and sticking little pegs in here and there.

'At the end of two yards,' she said, putting in a peg to mark the distance, 'I shall give you your directions.'

(*The Garden of Live Flowers*, T.L.G.)

'I wonder how many miles I've fallen by this time?' she said aloud. 'I must be getting somewhere near the centre of the earth. Let me see: that would be four thousand miles down, I think . . . yes, that's about the right distance—but then I wonder what Latitude or Longitude I've got to?'

(*Down the Rabbit-Hole*, A.A.W.)

Here the Red Queen began again. 'Can you answer useful questions?' she said. 'How is bread made?'

'I know *that*!' Alice cried eagerly. 'You take some flour——'

'Where do you pick the flower?' the White Queen asked: 'In a garden or in the hedges?'

'Well, it isn't *picked* at all,' Alice explained: 'it's ground——'

'How many acres of ground?' said the White Queen. 'You mustn't leave out so many things.'

(*Queen Alice*, T.L.G.)

Nonsense requires precision not merely in spatial but also in temporal relations.

> Robin and Richard
>   Were two pretty men;
> They lay in bed
>   Till the clock struck ten.

> Are the children in their beds,
>   For now it's eight o'clock?

So they remained there about six weeks, till they had eaten nearly all the fishes.

(*The Four Little Children*, N.S.B.)

Thus, in less than eighteen weeks, they all arrived safely at home.

(*Ibid.*)

G

Mr. and Mrs. Discobbolos
  Lived on the top of a wall,
For twenty years, a month and a day.

(L.L.)

But Carroll once again not only provides the information,
he states the need of knowing it exactly.

The Hatter was the first to break the silence. 'What day
of the month is it?' he said, turning to Alice: he had taken
his watch out of his pocket, and was looking at it uneasily,
shaking it every now and then, and holding it to his ear.
  Alice considered a little, and then said 'The fourth.'
  'Two days wrong!' sighed the Hatter.

(*A Mad Tea-Party*, A.A.W.)

'You ought to have finished,' said the King. 'When did
you begin?'
  The Hatter looked at the March Hare who had followed
him into court, arm-in-arm with the Dormouse. 'Four-
teenth of March, I *think* it was,' he said.
  'Fifteenth,' said the March Hare.
  'Sixteenth,' said the Dormouse.
  'Write that down,' the King said to the jury.

(*Who Stole the Tarts?*, A.A.W.)

The demand for exactitude in these matters can also take
the form of insistence on temporal order, on what is to
come first, second and third.

'No, no!' said the Queen. 'Sentence first—verdict
afterwards.'
  'Stuff and nonsense!' said Alice loudly. 'The idea of
having the sentence first!'

(*Who Stole the Tarts?*, A.A.W.)

'You don't know how to manage Looking-glass cakes,'
the Unicorn remarked. 'Hand it round first, and cut it
afterwards.'

(*The Lion and the Unicorn*, T.L.G.)

This last example looks as if the normal succession of things
were being tampered with; the same thing would hold

good of the scene in the *Garden of Live Flowers*, where Alice
finds she has to walk in the opposite direction to reach her
destination. Both these examples, however, take place in
the Looking-Glass, where the correct procedure is the reverse of normal. The series in reverse is none the less a
series. The three instances where time and succession as
they appear in real life are really upset, in the chapter
An Outlandish Watch in *Sylvie and Bruno*, are very unpleasant.

Similarly the cases in the Alices where time seems to
have got stuck are only examples of concentration on the
fixed rather than the fluctuating aspect of time and its
continuum. It is as if the characters try to stop at one of
the points where time and number are correlated; but it
is worth noticing that none of these affect Alice herself.
She retains the mobility necessary for the playing of a
game. The Hatter's tea-party may be fixed in a state 'in
which it seemed always afternoon', held in a permanent
condition of suspense 'because it's always six o'clock now',
but Alice can come and go as she pleases. In any case the
tea-party make up for their fixity in time by mobility in
space—'Let's all move one place on!' At the end of the
Looking-Glass, the White Queen talks about 'one of the
last set of Tuesdays' and says, 'Now *here*, we mostly have
days and nights two or three at a time, and sometimes in
the winter we take as many as five nights together.' This
again is merely a rearrangement of a series, producing a
different order but depending for its effect on the fact that
the mind is familiar with the original series, and can play
about with its units. In a sense the rearrangement insists
on the original order. The point is important in view of
the argument that there is an affinity between Nonsense
and dream. The main feature, as I take it, of space and
time in dreams is its instability, so that a thing can be in
two places at once, or can be two things at one and the
same time, the accent being on simultaneity, not on succession. The emphasis in the Alices is towards giving time
a greater controllability, at the direction of the will:—

'Seven years and six months!' Humpty Dumpty repeated thoughtfully. 'An uncomfortable sort of age. Now if you'd asked *my* advice, I'd have said "Leave off at seven"—but it's too late now.'

. . . she said, 'One can't help growing older.'

'One ca'n't, perhaps,' said Humpty Dumpty, 'but *two* can. With proper assistance, you might have left off at seven.'

The same principle is behind the Hatter's remark about time, 'Now, if you only kept on good terms with him, he'd do almost anything you liked with the clock.'

Infinity or the continuum are not the only problems for Nonsense, however. Indeed they could be regarded as a rather specialized problem as far as ordinary life is concerned, for most phenomena that occur collectively suggest multiplicity to the mind rather than infinitude. In Nonsense multiplicity no less than infinity will have to be limited and controlled by an insistence on the individuality of the group. Endless numbers of maids with an indefinite battery of mops will not avail to sweep out of the mind the sands of infinity. We must have a tidy team with a number, and the number of tools will be specified too, so that nothing may be left vague or indeterminate. The mind cannot in fact overcome infinity in this way, but at least it can be distracted by the introduction of certain definite numbers. A little further on in *Through the Looking-Glass* an apparently unmanageable multitude is reduced mentally to order by means of assigning to it an exact number. This is in the Lion and Unicorn chapter, where Alice meets the soldiers coming through the wood. They start by being within the framework of number: 'at first in twos and threes, then twenty or thirty together, and at last in such crowds that they seemed to fill the whole forest.' They threaten to turn into an unnumbered multitude, throwing off the controls of number altogether, and this produces in Alice a slight sense of danger. 'Alice got behind a tree, for fear of being run over, and watched them go by.' Not only are they slightly dangerous, however; they are also unwieldy and unstable, and this peculiarity of theirs leads straight into chaos:—

> She thought that in all her life she had never seen soldiers so uncertain on their feet: they were always tripping over something or other, and whenever one went down, several more always fell over him, so that the ground was soon covered with little heaps of men.
>
> Then came the horses. Having four feet, these managed rather better than the foot-soldiers; but even *they* stumbled now and then; and it seemed to be a regular rule that, whenever a horse stumbled, the rider fell off instantly. The confusion got worse every moment, and Alice was very glad to get out of the wood into an open place, where she found the White King seated on the ground, busily writing in his memorandum-book.

At this point the confusion has to be brought to order. The soldiers are not like the sand which would have baffled those seven maids with seven mops; they can be correlated with some point on the number scale, and need not be put in the infinite class which will remove them from the sphere of play altogether. So number is introduced, to control this multitude of things:—

> 'I've sent them all!' the King cried in a tone of delight, on seeing Alice. 'Did you happen to meet any soldiers, my dear, as you came through the wood?'
>
> 'Yes, I did,' said Alice: 'several thousand, I should think.'
>
> 'Four thousand two hundred and seven, that's the exact number,' the King said, referring to his book.

Here number and things are brought together, exactitude is given to a vague multiplicity, and the attention of the player is diverted from the potential infinity of each series to the precision set up by the union of a number and a collection of things. It is as if these two series were two lines on a graph, and the reader were invited to direct his attention solely to the point of intersection.

This works both ways. Nonsense not only calls in number to help define and limit an otherwise vague plurality, it also likes to add to the number a group of concrete and everyday things. It is as if the union of the two lent an added reliability to either side. Let number (which is only in the mind) be called in to allow the mind to master and manipulate collections of things; but let things also be firmly tacked on to number, lest the latter fly away into pure abstraction. Children when they are counting fists to see who is to be 'he' in a game do not count 'One, two, three, four . . .' on the understanding that the eighth fist so counted must be dropped. They say,

> One potato, two potato, three potato, four,
> Five potato, six potato, seven potato, more.

Songs dealing with number do not suggest that it is particularly amusing to be able to count from one to twelve; but that is exactly what the following type of song turns on, only here the numbers have things added to them:—

> One man went to mow,
> Went to mow a meadow,
>   One man and his dog,
> Went to mow a meadow.

> Two men went to mow,
> Went to mow a meadow,
>   Two men, one man and his dog,
> Went to mow a meadow.

> Three men went to mow . . .

and so on up to twelve. The same thing can be worked the other way round, counting downwards or backwards:—

> Ten little nigger boys
>   Going out to dine,
> One over-ate himself,
>   And then there were nine.

> Nine little nigger boys
>   Sitting on a gate,

One fell backwards,
   And then there were eight.

Ten green bottles hanging on the wall,
Ten green bottles hanging on the wall,
   And if one green bottle should accidentally fall,
There'd be nine green bottles a-hanging on the wall.

Nine green bottles . . .

There were two birds sat on a stone,
One flew away, and then there was one;
The other flew after and then there was none,
And so the poor stone was left all alone.

All these things, nigger boys, green bottles, stones, birds, men and a dog, are giving weight and personality to the numbers to which they are attached, and in this way numbers and things give stability to one another. It is not a process which is confined to Nonsense, for poetry makes good use of a combination of numbers and things, too:—

There were four apples on the bough,
Half gold, half red, that one might know
The blood was ripe inside the core.
                  (SWINBURNE, *August*)

Under the keel nine fathom deep,
From the land of mist and snow,
The Spirit slid: and it was he
That made the ship to go.
            (COLERIDGE, *The Ancient Mariner*)

The morning is flying on the wings of his age
And a hundred storks perch on the sun's right hand.
        (DYLAN THOMAS, *Deaths and Entrances*)

Poetry has none the less to be a little careful about the use of number, lest by over-precision it slip out of poetry into the matter-of-factness which is much nearer Nonsense, as in Wordsworth's much derided lines:—

I've measured it from side to side:
'Tis three feet long and two feet wide.

Nonsense does not have to worry about this, however. It

can be as precise as it pleases, and the result is a riot of
things and numbers in close conjunction:—

> Sing a song of sixpence,
>   A pocketful of rye,
> Four and twenty blackbirds,
>   Baked in a pie.

> Three blind mice,
> Three blind mice,
> See how they run . . .

> As I was going to Saint Ives,
> I met a man with seven wives,
> Every wife had seven sacks,
> Every sack had seven cats,
> Every cat had seven kits,
> Kits, cats, sacks and wives,
> How many were going to Saint Ives?

> The good old Duke of York,
> He had ten thousand men . . .

> Four and twenty tailors
> Went out to catch a snail . . .

Lear produces numbers of examples:—

> There was an old Person whose habits
> Induced him to feed upon rabbits;
> When he'd eaten eighteen, he turned perfectly
>   green,
> Upon which he relinquished those habits.
>
> (B.N.)

> Said the Duck, 'As I sate on the rocks,
>   I have thought over that completely,
> And I bought four pairs of worsted socks
>   Which fit my web-feet neatly.'
> (The Duck and the Kangaroo, N.S.B.)

They loaded the boat with two thousand veal-cutlets and
a million of chocolate drops. . . .
(The Four Little Children, N.S.B.)

After this they came to a shore where there were no less than sixty-five great red parrots with blue tails. . . .

(Ibid.)

Slingsby, Guy, and Lionel offered them three small boxes, containing respectively, Black Pins, Dried Figs, and Epsom Salts. . . .

(Ibid.)

There was an old man of the Dargle
Who purchased six barrels of Gargle . . .

(M.N.)

There was an old person of Minety
Who purchased five hundred and ninety
Large apples and pears, which he threw unawares
At the heads of the people of Minety.

(M.N.)

Carroll's verse contains a few examples, the maids and mops and oysters we have already met in *The Walrus and the Carpenter*, Father William's 'one shilling the box— Allow me to sell you a couple?', the White Knight's two-pence-halfpenny for the Rowland's Macassar-Oil. Carroll as usual produces fewer examples, but at the same time gives a comment on the particular Nonsense manœuvre that is going on. In *Looking-Glass Insects*, Alice finds herself in a railway carriage, while a chorus of voices keeps talking about a thousand pounds, till Alice says, 'I shall dream about a thousand pounds to-night, I know I shall!' Money is a very ordinary form of the connection between number and things (It is interesting that most of the above examples from Carroll are concerned with money.) Money provides a kind of tangible number scale against which things can be measured, and that is exactly what happens in this railway carriage scene. Carroll seems once again to be trying to make points of intersection between the number series in the form of money, and various other things, four of which are mentioned.

(1) 'Why, his time alone is worth a thousand pounds a
minute!'

(2) 'The land there is worth a thousand pounds an inch!'

(3) 'Why, the smoke alone is worth a thousand pounds a puff!'

(4) 'Language is worth a thousand pounds a word!'

They are split up by other oddments of conversation, but when put together they are remarkable, for they are then seen to be Time, Space, Things and Language. They are in each case something that appears to have tendencies towards indefiniteness, so each is split up into some kind of unit, a minute, an inch, a puff of smoke, a word, all of them small; and then as if to tie these down still further, they are correlated with a figure. Time and Space we have already dealt with; but there is more to be said yet about things and the attempt to keep them under control, and of course Language belongs here too.

Chapter 9

BATS AND TEA-TRAYS

S O F A R we have been looking at various ways in which number may be used in the game of Nonsense. Number, however, is only one expression of the mind's tendency towards order; beyond or behind it lies logic, the field of necessary relations between terms or groups of terms, and it is here rather than in the field of number that many games, chess in particular, belong. Collingwood, Carroll's nephew and biographer, relates that his uncle had the idea of a game in which letters could be moved about on a chess-board till they formed words. Chess and language seem to have been united in some way in Carroll's mind, as if it might be possible to manipulate words according to the principles of a game of chess, which are those of logic.

The creation of a possible and limited world from a series of combinations consisting of certain clearly defined units with specific functions, united by a minimum of necessary relations—this may be a comparatively straight-forward matter in chess. The Nonsense chess game, however, which takes place all through the Looking-Glass, is a continuous commentary on the difficulty of attaining such a result when the pieces are not chessmen but words. We have already seen that for things to be played with they have to be dead; and though words are not alive, Humpty Dumpty speaks of them in such a way: 'They've a temper, some of them—particularly verbs. . . . When I make a word do a lot of work like that, I always pay it extra.' This is part of the difficulty, for words, if they are to be played with, have to be prevented from working on the mind in other ways than those laid down by the rules of the game. Looked at in this way, the problem becomes one of relations. Chess and logic both depend on the establishment of a minimum of relations; one might at this point characterize order in the mind as economy of relations, disorder as multiplicity of relations. Words, the playthings of Nonsense, lend themselves quite as readily to disorder as to order. Relations between words and minds, and between mind and mind through the medium of words, are frequently complex and irrational. Nonsense cannot suppress this quality in words. All it can do is to attempt to keep down to a bare minimum the relations holding its word-combinations together. This is another side to the problem of creating a universe where things are one and one and one.

Nonsense has to make a simple universe from material which is complex and subject, in part at least, to a force whose main activity lies in weaving networks of relations, establishing associations, identifying one element with another and both with the mind in which this process is going on, observing strange and multiple likenesses, creating the never-stable complex which is the typical product of the dreaming mind. To prevent this happening, Nonsense can do only one thing: select and organize its words in such a way as to inhibit as far as possible the dreaming mind's tendency towards the multiplication of relations. The Nonsense universe must be the sum of its parts and nothing more. There must be no fusion and synthesis, no calling in of the dream faculty to lend to the whole so formed new significances beyond the grasp of logic. This will hold good at every level. Not only in the Nonsense universe viewed as a whole but in each unit employed in it, the emphasis must always be on the parts rather than the whole, on the ability of the whole to be broken down into parts again, on analysis, in fact. Part must be separate and distinct from part, wholes must be analysable into parts, and the total construction must be no more than a detached product of the conscious mind which must never identify itself with its production in any way.

The words which Nonsense is going to employ are those referring to normal experience, shoes and ships and sealing-wax and cabbages and kings. As we saw in Chapter 6, these words are themselves examples of wholes where there is no absolute and final unity, but the variability is reasonably well controlled. This type of word is the normal material of Nonsense, but it has the disadvantage that dream can also work upon these images of everyday life. Nonsense might have tried to get round this difficulty by using words which would give no purchase to dream, abstracts for instance which are too indistinct for dreams to get any grip on them. Such a method would be possible, and one of Carroll's sets of verses demonstrates it, those read at the trial of the Knave of Hearts:—

> . . . 'If I or she should chance to be
> Involved in this affair,
> He trusts to you to set them free,
> Exactly as we were.
>
> 'My notion was that you had been
> (Before she had this fit)
> · An obstacle that came between
> Him, and ourselves, and it.'

This is an isolated example, with its employment of pronouns, necessarily impersonal, and a complete sense of vacuum as far as the imaginative side of the mind is concerned. It shows, too, that Nonsense could not keep this up very long, or the mind would get bored, because it has nothing to play with. There is a halfway house between this and more ordinary forms of Nonsense in Humpty Dumpty's song. This has a number of things in it, little fishes, a kettle, the pump, bed, a corkscrew, but the vacuum is still there. There is a very similar example in Mr. A. A. Milne's *Winnie the Pooh*. These manœuvres are not really part of the game, however, for if Nonsense were to use only words which gave dream and disorder no chance to play, the game would collapse for want of an opponent. A game does not consist in removing oneself from the opponent's reach, but in overcoming him at his own game, and this is in general what Nonsense tries to do. It adopts the elements common to order and disorder in the mind,—words referring to concrete things in the world—and tries to keep disorder in play while it builds up with those elements a universe which will be orderly. Meantime it adopts certain safeguards so as not to make its task too difficult.

One of Carroll's verses will again provide an example. It is one of the parodies, and the changes made from the original are excellent indications of what Nonsense is trying to do. The original runs as follows:—

> Twinkle, twinkle, little <u>star</u>,
> How I wonder what you are!
> Up above the world so high,
> Like a dia<u>m</u>ond in the sky!
> (From *Rhymes for the Nursery* by JANE TAYLOR)

Carroll, by the mouth of the Mad Hatter, makes this of it:—

> Twinkle, twinkle, little bat!
> How I wonder what you're at!
> Up above the world you fly,
> Like a tea-<u>tray</u> in the sky.

A number of things have happened here. A bat has been substituted for a star, a tea-tray for a diamond; the bat is twinkling and the tray is up in the sky; a bat is likened to a tea-tray. The problem is first one of selection, then of organization, as we saw in Chapter 6. What is there about bats and tea-trays that makes them more suitable for Nonsense than stars and diamonds, and why are they combined in this particular way?

Stars and bats, to take the first substitution, are both objects in the world of experience. In that respect the references of the words are similar, and they are both potential material for order or disorder. It is the differences in the reference which are important, however. A star is something exceedingly remote and beyond control; it has no apparent parts and can be assigned by the ordinary observer no definite qualities other than those of size and degree of brightness; it is beautiful, according to the Scholastic definition: 'beautiful things are those which please when seen'; it is one of an unnumbered multitude. A bat is something near at hand, reasonably familiar, small; it is a creature whose appearance and habits are familiar; it is grotesque and we feel no attraction towards it; it usually appears alone. The other substitution, that of a tea-tray for a diamond, works on much the same principles, abandoning beauty, rarity, preciousness and attraction for ordinariness. It adds one further distinction, for a tea-tray is the work of man. In other words, the artificial is here preferred to the work of nature. Smallness, ordinariness, artificiality, distinctness of units, and a tendency to concentrate on the part rather than the whole are all helpful in the playing of Nonsense. It is with these qualities that we live our daily lives, and they characterize our familiar surroundings, clothes, food, furniture and houses and so on. Nonsense plays with all of these in the mind.

We will take clothes first. Lear pays much attention to what his characters wear, and describes it in detail:—

> There was a young person in red,
> Who carefully covered her head
> With a bonnet of leather, and three lines
>   of feather,
> Besides some long ribands of red.
>
> (M.N.)

> The Kicking Kangaroo,
> who wore a Pale Pink Muslin dress
> with Blue spots.
>
> (M.N.)

. . . a particularly odious little boy, dressed in rose-coloured knickerbockers, and with a pewter plate upon his head . . .

(*The Four Little Children*, N.S.B.)

There was an Old Man in a pew,
Whose waistcoat was spotted with blue;
But he tore it in pieces, to give to his nieces,
That cheerful Old Man in a pew.

(B.N.)

The last of these examples is a model of Nonsense procedure: an individual in a small and limited place, clad
in a particular fashion which is described, the garment in
question being later torn up (the whole broken down into
parts) and distributed to a well-defined and numerically
limited group of people. The need for precision in these
matters comes into *Through the Looking-Glass:*—

> 'What a beautiful belt you've got on!' Alice suddenly
> remarked. . . . 'At least,' she corrected herself on second
> thoughts, 'a beautiful cravat, I should have said—no, a
> belt, I mean—I beg your pardon!' she added in dismay,
> for Humpty Dumpty looked thoroughly offended. . . .
> 'It is a—*most—provoking*—thing,' he said at last, 'when a
> person doesn't know a cravat from a belt!'

Poetry, too, is apt to describe certain types of clothing:—

> When we came in by Glasgow town,
>   We were a comely sight to see:
> My Love was clad in the black velvet
>   And I myself in cramasie.
> (*O Waly, Waly up the Bank*)

> The king's daughter is all glorious within: her clothing is of
> wrought gold.
>   She shall be brought unto the king in raiment of needle-
> work. . . .
> (PSALM xlv)

But Nonsense adds to poetry's precision an element of incongruity; in the examples quoted above it can be seen
that there is to be no fittingness or unity between clothes
and wearer, or between one part of a garment and
another. The following is typical of this:—

There was an Old Man of the West,
Who wore a pale plum-coloured vest;
When they said, 'Does it fit?' he replied, 'Not a bit!
That uneasy Old Man of the West.

(B.N.)

So is the White Knight, who was 'dressed in tin armour, which seemed to fit him very badly'. There is precision and distinction of parts, as in poetry, but no inner relationship is allowed to develop between them in the mind.

The same thing happens to food. If a whole is given, parts are enumerated, and parts which do not fit: 'it had, in fact, a sort of mixed flavour of cherry-tart, custard, pineapple, roast turkey, toffee, and hot buttered toast' (*Down the Rabbit-Hole*, A.A.W.). Requests for precision on this point occur frequently:—

'What did they live on?' said Alice, who always took a great interest in questions of eating and drinking.
'They lived on treacle,' said the Dormouse. . . .
(*A Mad Tea-Party*, A.A.W.)

'What does it live on?' Alice asked, with great curiosity.
'Sap and sawdust,' said the Gnat. . . .
'And what does *it* live on?'
'Weak tea with cream in it.'
(*Looking-Glass Insects*, T.L.G.)

'And yet it was a very clever pudding to invent.'
'What did you mean it to be made of?' Alice asked.
'It began with blotting-paper,' the Knight answered with a groan.
'That wouldn't be very nice, I'm afraid——'
'Not very nice *alone*,' he interrupted, quite eagerly: 'but you've no idea what a difference it makes, mixing it with other things—such as gunpowder and sealing-wax.'
(*'It's My Own Invention'*, T.L.G.)

. . . 'but if we may take the liberty of enquiring, on what do you chiefly subsist?'
'Mainly on Oyster-patties,' said the Blue-bottle Fly,

H

'and, when these are scarce, on Raspberry Vinegar and Russian leather boiled down to a jelly.'

(LEAR, *The Four Little Children*, N.S.B.)

The Owls anxiously looked after mice, which they caught and made into sago puddings.

The Guinea Pigs toddled about the gardens, and ate lettuces and Cheshire cheese.

The Cats sat still in the sunshine, and fed upon sponge biscuits.

(*The Seven Families*, N.S.B.)

Lear produces the old man who drank warm brandy and soy, the Jumblies eating dumplings made with yeast, the Owl and the Pussy-Cat having mince and slices of quince for their dinner, the old person who fed on roast spiders and chutney taken with tea, another eating underdone veal, another whose provender was cold apple tart. Lear's Nonsense cookery belongs here too, alongside the White Knight's recipe for a pudding, these being excellent examples of a whole being considered merely as the sum of its parts; but these parts are incapable of making a whole, and Lear more or less admits this at the end of his recipe for Gosky Patties: 'Ascertain if at the end of that period the whole is about to turn into Gosky Patties. If it does not then, it never will; and in that case the Pig may be let loose, and the whole process may be considered as finished' (N.S.B.).

Furniture, houses, and all the artificial paraphernalia of man's existence meet with the same treatment. We know what the Jumblies' boat was made of—a sieve, a crockery jar and a tobacco-pipe mast; the details of the material and construction of the Dong's luminous nose are supplied, and the furnishings of the court are given:—

> And if you went, you'd see such sights!
> Such rugs! and jugs! and candle-lights!
> And more than all, the King and Queen,
> One in red, and one in green!
>
> (*The Daddy Long-Legs and the Fly*, N.S.B.)

The March Hare's house has a roof thatched with fur, and one remembers the house in Hänsel and Gretel, made of sugar pastries. Even the body can be treated in this way sometimes, as if it too were a conglomeration of elements of which a list can be given:—

> What are little boys made of?
> What are little boys made of?
>   Slugs and snails and puppydogs' tails—
> That's what little boys are made of!

This Nursery Rhyme does not substitute an artificiality for a real being, but it suggests that the latter is after all only a conglomeration of incongruous things, of which a list can be given, and the emphasis is on the constituents rather than on the organic whole, because the works of nature are not very suitable for playthings, and a wooden mallet is better than a flamingo when it comes to dealing with a croquet ball. So whenever the works of creation occur in Nonsense they tend to be safeguarded in one of several ways. This procedure that we have just seen is one of them. It can also be seen in one of Belloc's rhymes— indeed his Nonsense collections, *The Bad Child's Book of Beasts* and *More Beasts for Worse Children*, are excellent examples of this branch of Nonsense work, for beasts are undoubtedly real and living, and he has to deal with them carefully to make them suitable for Nonsense. Here, for instance, is the suggestion that they are artificially made:—

> The Bison is vain,
> And I write it with pain—
>   The doormat you see on his head
> Is not, as some learned professors maintain,
> The opulent growth of a genius brain,
>   But is sewn on with needle and thread.

Carroll's Looking-Glass insects are made of wood, holly-leaves, lumps of sugar, Lear's plants of dinner-bells and nutmeg-graters. The crabs in Lear's *Four Little Children* have detachable claws (' "They are all made to unscrew", said the Crabs') and in Wonderland there is an attempt to transform a white into a red rose tree by means of red paint. So the insistence on at least partial artificiality is preserved. A second safeguard is that the creatures which appear in Nonsense are usually only one of a kind. The change in the *How doth the little* parody from a bee to a crocodile may perhaps suggest this. Bees are readily thought of as part of a swarm, while a crocodile, rightly or wrongly, seems a good deal more individual. It is noticeable how in Wonderland the creatures which Alice meets are singulars: a white rabbit, a mouse, 'a Duck and a Dodo, a Lory and an Eaglet' (*The Pool of Tears*), a lizard, a caterpillar, a cat and so on. Occasionally a pair of creatures is introduced, for instance the two guinea-pigs who revive Bill the Lizard; but on the other hand normal pairs are sometimes curtailed:—

> I passed by his garden, and marked, with one eye,
> How the Owl and the Panther were sharing a pie.
> (*The Lobster-Quadrille*, A.A.W.)

Perhaps that is why, in Nonsense, one egg is more valuable than two: 'Fivepence farthing for one—twopence for two' (*Wool and Water*, T.L.G.). One further obvious method of endowing creatures with artificiality is to ascribe human attributes to them.

> A python I should not advise:
> It needs a doctor for its eyes,
>   And has the measles yearly.
>
> (BELLOC)

Humpty Dumpty is an egg dressed up, just as the white rabbit has a waistcoat and a watch, gloves and a fan. The caterpillar smokes a hookah, and Lear's Duck smokes a cigar. The Lobster is heard complaining, 'You have baked me too brown, I must sugar my hair'; Lear's Pelican wears a wreath in hers. And all the animals, birds, insects and even plants can talk, to complete the picture of the human and voluntary superimposed on the instinctive and animal to make it more controllable for Nonsense.

These are all minor points; but behind them lies something of real importance, the strict avoidance of beauty in Nonsense. Beauty has a double danger for Nonsense, and once again St. Thomas can help us to discover why. He relates beauty to goodness and says that the essence of goodness is that it is desirable, and that love in some way unites the lover and the thing loved (*Summa*, Pt. I—II, Q. 27, Art. 1; Pt. I, Q.5, Art. 1; Pt. I—II, Q. 28, Art. 1). If this is so, it suggests that beauty invites the mind of the beholder to some kind of union with the beautiful object. This is a tendency towards fusion; the beholder's detachment and indifference are no longer intact, and the dream side of the mind begins to come into play. There are two passages in the Alices which form an interesting commentary on just this process, for in them beauty is allowed by the author to enter into the narrative, and at once the atmosphere of the work is impaired and the passages threaten to break the fabric of the Nonsense universe. Both occur in *Through the Looking-Glass*, the first in *Wool and Water* where Alice gathers the scented rushes, the second when she says goodbye to the White Knight. Such descriptions of attractive surroundings are very dangerous in the circumstances, and it is significant that both these passages contain a reference to dream:—

> These, being dream-rushes, melted away almost like snow, as they lay in heaps at her feet.

> All this she took in like a picture, as, with one hand shading her eyes, she leant against a tree, watching the strange pair, and listening, in a half-dream, to the melancholy music of the song.

In each passage the dream almost wins, but the writer recovers himself just in time to save his world from disruption by the forces admitted by beauty.

The second danger that beauty has for Nonsense lies in this, that 'beauty consists in due proportion' (*Summa*, Pt. I,

Q. 5, Art. 4). This may be taken to mean that each part of any whole must be fitting in relation to the other parts and to the whole itself. The mind perceives this kind of proportion in the works of creation, and this is another reason why the latter are dangerous for Nonsense. They have a way of impressing the mind as organisms rather than organizations. Nonsense is bound to quarrel with this and so proposes rearrangements or exaggerates one element at the expense of the whole, so that the emphasis shall be thrown back on the parts and the relations between them rather than on the whole which might strike the mind too forcibly as a self-sufficient and possibly beautiful and lovable being. Humpty Dumpty provides a good example:—

'That's just what I complain of,' said Humpty Dumpty. 'Your face is the same as everybody has—the two eyes, so—' (marking their places in the air with his thumb) 'nose in the middle, mouth under.   It's always the same. Now if you had the two eyes on the same side of the nose, for instance—or the mouth at the top—that would be *some* help.'

Humpty is complaining about the difficulty of identifying people, and demurs when Alice protests that his suggested alteration would not look nice. Nonsense could hardly state more clearly that it is perfectly prepared to sacrifice attractiveness for more precise differentiation.

One way of upsetting an impression of unity is to rearrange the parts. Another way is to distort or exaggerate one part. A third is to expand or contract the whole in contrast with its usual surroundings, taking a slightly larger unit and upsetting the unity there. The parts of the body are an obvious place to begin.

There was a Young Lady whose nose
Was so long that it reached to her toes;

There was an Old Man of the South
Who had an immoderate mouth;

There was a Young Lady whose eyes
Were unique as to colour and size;

(B.N.)

Lear and Carroll both have a character with a very
pointed chin:—

There was a Young Lady whose chin
Resembled the point of a pin;
So she had it made sharp, and purchased a harp,
And played several tunes with her chin.

(B.N.)

She was exactly the right height to rest her chin on
Alice's shoulder, and it was an uncomfortably sharp chin.
(*The Mock-Turtle's Story*, A.A.W.)

In both authors the hair of the head gets exaggerated:—

'First you take an upright stick,' said the Knight.
'Then you make your hair creep up it, like a fruit-tree.'
('*It's My Own Invention*', T.L.G.)

There was a young lady of Firle,
Whose hair was addicted to curl;
It curled up a tree, and all over the sea,
That expansive young lady of Firle.

(M.N.)

Lear has several beings with immensely long legs, and at
one point in Alice's transformations in Wonderland she
acquires a long serpentine neck. The disproportion spreads
over into man-made things as well. Lear's Old Man at
Deeside has a huge hat under which people can shelter
from hail. The Old Person of Blythe cuts up his meat with
a scythe. The White Knight's helmet is so big that he can
fall right into it; Uncle Arly's shoes on the other hand are
'far too tight' (N.S.S.), for disproportion can work both
ways, towards diminution as well as exaggeration, and we
have the person of Dutton 'whose head was so small as a
button' (B.N.). Alice herself is sometimes unduly big and
sometimes unduly small compared with her surroundings,
and this happens to other things too.

There was an Old Man who said 'Hush!
I perceive a young bird in this bush!'
When they said—'Is it small?' He replied—
  'Not at all!
It is four times as big as the bush!'

(B.N.)

In the landscape described at the beginning of *Looking-Glass Insects* the bees have become as large as elephants, and the flowers are enlarged to the same size; but Alice is not. Lear has enormous bees too:—

There was an old person of Dover,
Who rushed through a field of blue clover;
But some very large bees, stung his nose and
  his knees,
So he very soon went back to Dover.

(B.N.)

Another old man has his garments eaten by 'some very large rats'. Belloc has a greatly enlarged Microbe:—

His jointed tongue that lies beneath
A hundred curious rows of teeth,
His eyebrows of a tender green—
All these have never yet been seen,

but his crocodile, which one normally thinks of as a sizeable beast, is small:—

. . . he found his egg contain,
Green, hungry, horrible and plain,
  An infant crocodile.

So Carroll's, too, is 'the little crocodile'.

It is not only by words that this disproportion and deliberate absence of unity is insisted on. It is done by the drawings as well; sometimes the words say nothing of an exaggeration which the illustration makes clear. A typical example is Lear's limerick:—

There was an old person of Skye,
Who waltz'd with a Bluebottle fly:
They buzz'd a sweet tune, to the light of the
  moon,
And entranced all the people of Skye.

Lear has drawn the fly as big as the man, and the two
look very like one another. It may be as well to consider
at this point the use of illustrations in Nonsense, for they
are an interesting example of how Nonsense sets out to
defeat the dream and disorder force in the mind on its own
ground. It is a fact of experience that dreams are almost
entirely visual in character; and so one of the Nonsense
ways of defeating dream is to pick up the latter's principal
elements, images, and use them for its own ends. We have
seen how careful Nonsense is to create its world from
images of concrete everyday things. Here it goes one stage
further, and employs actual images, pictures in black and
white before the eye. M. Cammaerts remarks on the fact
that Nonsense writers seem always to want to illustrate
their work: 'We are led to think that there is more than a
coincidence in the fact that nonsense writers are also nonsense draughtsmen' (*op. cit.*, p. 60). Lear did all his own
drawings, as well he might, being a professional artist; but
it is perhaps not so well known that Carroll also illustrated
himself the first version of *Alice's Adventures in Wonderland*,
and although he later employed artists to do his illustrations, he exercised an exceedingly close, not to say tyran-
nical, supervision over them. Gilbert, Belloc, Chesterton
and T. H. White have all illustrated their Nonsense themselves. This suggests that the illustrations are not just
adornment to the Nonsense letterpress, but serve a special
purpose of their own, and are as relevant to the author's
aims as the words. To provide the mind with actual images
in addition to those mental ones called up by the words
employed might seem to give an advantage to the dream
force in the mind, providing it with more immediate
material on which to work its characteristic transformation. In fact the contrary is the case. Illustrations store the
mind with images, it is true, but those images are fixed by
the illustrator, and where the latter is doing the writing
as well, he has a dual control over the reader's mind. The
aim of Nonsense is to inhibit one half of the mind, and

nothing more hinders the dream or imagination than to
have its pictures provided. It is common experience to read
a narrative which has been illustrated and find oneself
completely unable to visualize the people and happenings
in any other way, even though one may not care for the
illustrations given, and would prefer one's own imaginings.
The providing of pictures is a regular part of the Nonsense
game. They sterilize the mind's powers of invention and
combination of images while seeming to nourish it, and by
precision and detail they contribute towards detachment
and definition of the elements of the Nonsense universe.

There is one other point to consider in this chapter, not
unlike the above, another daring sally which Nonsense
makes into dream territory, giving it material which is
apparently suitable to the dreaming faculty and then in-
hibiting its function. This is the last of the points arising
from *Twinkle, twinkle*—the comparison of a bat to a tea-
tray. The employment of likeness and similitude is a
normal characteristic of dream. Poetry knows this well,
and since it is poetry's nature to employ dream principles
for the construction of its reference side, it makes full use
of simile, metaphor, imagery and figurative speech of all
kinds, where things are likened to other things and at
times identified with them. This type of concentration on
an underlying and occult unity among phenomena, created
by a multiplicity of irrational relations and perceived by
the dream faculty of the mind, is fatal to Nonsense which
must keep its universe strictly analytical and economize
in relations as far as possible. As before, however, Nonsense does not refuse to provide its adversary with material;
it suggests likenesses, but these turn out to be of such a
kind that the mind cannot, rationally or irrationally, fuse
them into unity.

In the original of *Twinkle, twinkle*, a star is compared to
a diamond. The image is a trite one in poetry, but is none
the less legitimate, for the mind can fuse stars and diamonds
without difficulty and can take a characteristic dream-

pleasure in so doing. Carroll puts in place of this a comparison between a bat and a tea-tray. The dream side of the mind can do nothing with this at all, and that is as it should be in Nonsense. There is another excellent example of the same thing at the Mad Hatter's tea-party, where the Hatter proposes to Alice the riddle: Why is a Raven like a Writing-desk? She considers this for some time.

> 'Have you guessed the riddle yet?' the Hatter said, turning to Alice again.
> 'No, I give it up,' Alice replied. 'What's the answer?'
> 'I haven't the slightest idea,' said the Hatter.
> 'Nor I,' said the March Hare.

Alice is cross at what she feels to be a waste of time; but it is essential for Nonsense that the riddle should have no solution. It is propounded to keep the dream and disorder side of the mind in play, but there must be no answer which could set up some kind of unity between the parts. Nonsense provides other examples:—

> 'You see the wind is very strong here. It's as strong as soup.'   (*'It's My Own Invention'*, T.L.G.)

> Let us take them in order. The first is the taste,
>   Which is meagre and hollow, but crisp:
> Like a coat that is rather too tight in the waist,
>   With a flavour of Will-o'-the-Wisp.
>   (*The Hunting of the Snark*)
> Like the ancient Medes and Persians,
> Always by his own exertions,
>   He subsisted on those hills.
>   (LEAR, *Incidents in the Life of My Uncle Arly*, N.S.S.)

Lear keeps most of his comparisons for his drawings. The Old Man of Dunblane who greatly resembled a crane is shown in detail, as is the old man of West Dumpet who possessed a large nose like a trumpet; indeed the old man's nose quite plainly *is* a trumpet, and the incongruity of the combination, fixed and held down by the picture, covers up the fact that a likeness has been introduced. The same thing happens in the case of the old person of Cassel, whose nose finished off in a tassel:

> But they call'd out, 'Oh well!—don't it look like a bell!'
> Which perplexed that old person of Cassel.

The odd assemblage of elements and the distortion of one feature preserve the separateness of the units so that the mind can still play with them, and the dream faculty, though potentially called in by the simile, cannot operate.

All the finer points of the Nonsense game which we have seen so far contribute to the main aim: to create a universe which will be logical and orderly, with separate units held together by a strict economy of relations, not subject to dream and disorder with its multiplication of relationships and associations. 'And what is the height and ideal of mere association?' Coleridge asks, and answers, 'Delirium'.[1] Nonsense is so far removed from delirium just because it takes infinite pains to prevent associations forming in the mind. From the dangerous ground of stars and diamonds we are led to bats and tea-trays, and so by means of separateness and distinctness in the elements and the particular nature of their combinations in Nonsense, we avoid poetry first, then dream, then delirium and madness. Like Hamlet, our proof of sanity in this universe which might so well be lunatic is that we know, not a hawk from a handsaw, but a bat from a tea-tray when the wind is in the right quarter.

[1] From *Anima Poetæ*, from the Unpublished Note-Books of Samuel Taylor Coleridge, edited by Ernest Hartley Coleridge, Heinemann, London, 1895, p. 56.

Chapter 10

THE BALANCE OF BRILLIG

W E H A V E made by now what amounts to a general inventory of the paraphernalia of the world of Nonsense. No matter where you break into that world, you are liable to find something like the surroundings of the Yonghy-Bonghy-Bò, to take a typical example—pumpkins, two old chairs and half a candle, shrimps and watercress, Dorking hens, a jug without a handle, a hat which blows off. There are other things in this small world as well, however, and it is to these we must now turn. First of all there is the Bò himself, the Bong-trees among which he lives, the places named—the isles of Boshen, the Bay of Gurtle, and so on. We have seen already the great care with which Nonsense chooses its words and the things it will talk about. The Jabberwock vocabulary, the Nonsense neologisms, can scarcely be said to be words, since words should have reference but these have none, making no direct connection for the mind with anything in experience. We have to see what part they play in Nonsense; but, to judge by the pattern that has come to light so far, the odds are that their function will be as exact and controlled as the rest. Their coining may have been the result of a stroke of genius, a sudden flash of intuition or a kind of mental or verbal effervescence; but that need not mean that their role in Nonsense is casual or unimportant.

The most concentrated example of this type of vocabulary is, of course, *Jabberwocky*, probably Carroll's most famous piece of work; and this will serve as our guide here, just as other Carroll verses have done earlier. It might seem as though, in dealing with these verses, we were on rather easier ground, since they are given an explanation, at some length, by Humpty Dumpty. Further, Carroll

himself in the Preface to *The Hunting of the Snark* gives a
commentary on Humpty Dumpty's commentary, and later
criticism has tended to take on from there. It is quite
possible, however, that the most helpful approach to Nonsense words may lie elsewhere in the books, and have to be
teased out. *Jabberwocky* is not by any means the only
ground for research. Lear has a very fine collection of
Nonsense words, and anyone interested in the scope of the
problem will find it set out in Mr. Eric Partridge's essay
on *The Nonsense Words of Edward Lear and Lewis Carroll* in
Here, There and Everywhere. Most Nonsense writers invent
terms from time to time. Belloc has the Wanderoo:—

> Or why the Wanderoo should rant
> In wild unmeaning rhymes,
> Or why the Indian Elephant
> Will only read The Times.

A. A. Milne has 'wild woozles who inhabit the North Pole'.
There are various other verbal manœuvres too, which are
a feature of Nonsense and which we may as well consider
here, the transplantation of words out of their proper
context, for instance, or the use of compounds.

It is important to take a fairly wide field, because the
authoritarian Humpty Dumpty, backed up later by Carroll himself, has suggested an over-simple explanation.
Humpty Dumpty undertakes to interpret the hard words,
says that *brillig* is four o'clock in the afternoon, when you
start broiling things for dinner, and then goes on to *slithy*
which he maintains is a combination of lithe and slimy:
'You see—it's like a portmanteau—there are two meanings packed up into one word.' To this Carroll adds in the
Snark Preface: 'Humpty Dumpty's theory, of two meanings packed into one word like a portmanteau, seems to
me the right explanation of all.' As Mr. Partridge points
out, this is no explanation of genuine inventions such as
the *Jubjub*, or Lear's *Moppsikon-Floppsikon*. Alice herself
seems reassuringly sceptical, for to Humpty's suggestion

about *brillig* she replies, 'Yes, that will do very well,' which implies a good deal of reserve or at least the understanding that a number of other interpretations would do equally well. There is a more interesting remark earlier in the conversation, and it may be as well to start here rather than with the portmanteau theory. Alice and Humpty have been having a difference of opinion about the noun 'glory', to which Humpty attributes an entirely personal meaning. When Alice complains, Humpty says that he intends to be master in his own house, and continues with the remark that adjectives are pliable and verbs tough. 'They've a temper, some of them—particularly verbs: they're the proudest—adjectives you can do anything with, but not verbs.' It is certain that in Nonsense vocabulary <u>nouns</u> and <u>adjectives</u> play by far the biggest part. Mr. Partridge in his classification of the vocabulary of *Jabberwocky* gives four new verbs, *gimble, outgrabe, galumphing* and *chortled*, to ten new adjectives and eight new nouns. In the list of Lear's neologisms the proportions are even more marked, with over two pages of new nouns and a page of adjectives to six verbs and one adverb.

It is worth noticing at the beginning that it is possible to classify Nonsense words into the normal grammatical categories. This is something we take very much for granted with Lear and Carroll, but it need not necessarily be so. For example, no classification is possible in this bit of Lear gibberish:—

> There was an old man of Spithead,
> Who opened the window, and said—
> 'Fil-jomble, fil-jumble, Fil-rumble-come-tumble!'
> That doubtful old man of Spithead.
>
> (M.N.)

any more than in the ballad refrain 'Hi diddle inkum feedle!' Nonsense inventions which are to serve as nouns and which might be hard to identify in isolation, *dong* for instance, or *rath*, are given their context carefully, either by a definite or indefinite article, or by means of adjectives

or other attributes: 'the dong with a luminous nose', or
'the mome raths'. Very often, too, they are given capital
letters. The adjectives are nearly always recognizable by
a typical adjectival suffix: *tulgey*, *uffish*, *manxome*, or Lear's
scroobious and *borascible*. The verbs follow the same lines,
and where form alone would be insufficient indication,
syntax makes the word's function clear.

We can assume that the writers wanted their sentences
containing Nonsense words to look like genuine sentences
bearing reference, and that they found nouns and adjectives better for their purpose than verbs. If Nonsense words
are to appear to be one of a class, it must be in order that
they should carry conviction as words rather than gibberish. *Brillig*, *Cloxam*, *Willeby-Wat* have no more reference
than *Hey nonny no* or *Hi diddle diddle*, but they seem to have,
because they are presented to us as nouns or adjectives,
and remind us of other words which have reference. As
regards the preference for nouns and adjectives over verbs,
it is interesting that Mallarmé, that most logical of poets,
should have shared it to a marked degree. (*Vide* Jacques
Scherer, *L'Expression Littéraire dans l'Œuvre de Mallarmé*,
Droz, Paris, 1947, pp. 87–113). In logic, a verb ex-
presses a relation, and this suggests two reasons for the few
invented verbs in Nonsense. The first is the impossibility
of inventing new relations in logic. The second is that a
verb is an expressed relation, and relations in logic have
to be simple and exact. If a Nonsense verb is invented, the
mind can only deal with it as it deals with Nonsense words
in general: it will produce from its memory all the other
words the neologism resembles, and this will multiply
relationships and associations in a manner quite alien to
the operation of logic. The latter is concerned with implied
relations between certain data, and it is well, therefore,
to keep the expressed relations as simple as possible, since
they are the groundwork. The verbs have to be simple
because they are important. The terms and the nature of
them, i.e. in this case nouns and adjectives, are, as we have

seen, much less important to the working of the system, and so they can be played with to a much greater degree. An example from Carroll's *Symbolic Logic* will illustrate the point:—

(1) No kitten, that loves fish, is unteachable;
(2) No kitten without a tail will play with a gorilla;
(3) Kittens with whiskers always love fish;
(4) No teachable kitten has green eyes;
(5) No kittens have tails unless they have whiskers.

We can move on now to an example of Nonsense wording; a very short one will do to start with:—

> . . . and shun
> The frumious Bandersnatch.

The verb is simple and familiar; we are left with a noun and an adjective. Humpty Dumpty's commentary on the poem does not go beyond the first verse, but the similar phrase, 'the slithy toves' is dealt with as follows: 'Well, "*slithy*" means "lithe and slimy" . . . "*toves*" are something like badgers—they're something like lizards—and they're something like corkscrews.' The noun is treated as if it were a technical term, a label and no more, and is invested at once with Nonsense properties of the kind we have observed in the last few chapters. The adjective is an example of Humpty Dumpty's portmanteau, and *frumious* is of the same type. Carroll says of it in the Snark Preface that it is a combination of 'fuming' and 'furious'. To take the adjectives first, *slithy* and *frumious*, it seems curious that Humpty Dumpty should have got by so easily on his portmanteau theory, for when one looks at it, it becomes very unsatisfactory. It would fit a pun well enough, in which there are precisely that—two meanings (or more than two) packed up in one word. But *frumious*, for instance, is not a word, and does not have two meanings packed up in it; it is a group of letters without any meaning at all. What Humpty Dumpty may have meant, but fails to say, is that it looks like two words, 'furious' and 'fuming', reminding

I

us of both simultaneously. It is not a word, but it looks like other words, and almost certainly more than two. In the examples given below one can see the sort of thing that happens, for each mind will vary in the particular words recalled by these Nonsense formations. I give Mr. Partridge's, from *Here, There and Everywhere*, and my own.

FRUMIOUS:

> *Carroll:* furious, fuming.
> *Partridge:* frumpish, gloomy.
> *Myself:* fume, with a connection with French *brume* and English *brumous*, frumenty, rheumy.

BANDERSNATCH

> *Partridge:* bandog, (?) *Bandar*, from Hindustani, snatching proclivities.
> *Myself:* Banshee and bandbox.

BORASCIBLE:

> *Partridge:* irascible, boring.
> *Myself:* Boreas, boracic, connection with Eastern Europe, through, I think, the prefix 'Bor', as in General Bor-Komorowski.

STAR-BESPRINGLED:

> *Partridge:* bespangled and besprinkled.
> *Myself:* connection with 'tingled', through the Tennysonian line: 'A cry that shivered to the tingling stars'; the name 'Pringle', connecting with dressmaking (? through a story), also perhaps 'pinprick'.

MOPPSIKON-FLOPPSIKON BEAR:

> *Partridge:* 'with a great *mop* of hair and a *floppy* gait?'
> *Myself:* Connection with Russia, through the 'ikon' ending. (Cf. Partridge's comment on 'Soffsky-Poffsky trees': 'of Siberian habitat?')

These are not intended as interpretations. They merely show that these words, though possessing no meaning themselves, remind the reader of many words which have reference. Nonsense words which do not act in this way, *Jubjub*, for instance, must have their function as technical terms made clear at once, and this in fact is what happens:

Beware the Jubjub bird . . .

(T.L.G.)

Should we meet with a Jubjub, that desperate bird,
We shall need all our strength for the job!

(H.S.)

On the whole, however, the first of these two forms is the commoner, a Nonsense word reminding the mind of other words which it resembles. It is important, for if a word does not look like a word, so to speak, the mind will not play with it. Carroll coins examples of this sort, *Mhruxian* and *grurmstipths* from *Tangled Tales* or the 'occasional exclamation' of the Gryphon, *Hjckrrh*, from *The Mock Turtle's Story*. Words such as these do not interest the mind; but dongs and toves look strangely familiar, and the mind can enjoy itself with them. Mr. Partridge has some delightful examples, making Lear's *Gramblamble* into *Grand Lama? grand brambles?* or Carroll's *Ipwergis* pudding from *Sylvie and Bruno* into *Walpurgis* and *haggis*. We are left with a half-conscious perception of verbal likenesses, and, in consequence, the evocation of a series of words.

It looks as if Nonsense were running on to dangerous ground here, for two of its rules are (*a*) no likenesses are to be observed, and (*b*) no trains of association are to be set up. At this point we shall have to go back to the Snark Preface for a moment, for, although we have rejected Carroll's suggestion that Humpty Dumpty's theory will cover all the Nonsense words, making the portmanteau into an umbrella, there is an interesting remark a little later on. Discussing the alternative of saying 'fuming-furious' or 'furious-fuming', Carroll says, 'but if you have that rarest of gifts, a perfectly balanced mind, you will say "frumious".' It is a hint that here as elsewhere Nonsense is maintaining some kind of balance in its language.[1] After all, Humpty Dumpty who is the chief language expert in the *Alices* is himself in such a state; Carroll could have made any of his characters discourse upon words, and it is interesting that the one who in fact does so was 'sitting, with his legs crossed like a Turk, on the top of a high wall—such a narrow one that Alice quite wondered how he could keep his balance'. What is the nature of this balance where Nonsense words are concerned, and why is it precarious?

One might suppose the danger to be that these Nonsense words break two important rules of the Nonsense game. In fact, however, this infringement is only apparent. We have seen already that although Nonsense plays on the side of order, its aim and method is to defeat disorder with disorder's own weapons. It allows disorder in the mind a certain amount of selected material apparently suitable for dream purposes (images and so on), and in this way draws the disordering faculty into play, but manages never to let it gain control. Exactly the same thing is happening here. The mind is encouraged by means of these Nonsense words to notice likenesses; but the likenesses are to other *words*. It is the purely verbal memory and associative faculty which is called into play. The danger for Nonsense is that likenesses perceived between images may run together into a poetic and dreaming unity; this almost happens with Lear's 'star-bespringled' for instance, but Nonsense words must in general avoid anything of this kind. To take another example, Lear's *Pobble* suggest to Mr. Partridge poodle and wabble, to myself bobble and pebble. Each of us has two good words plus the Nonsense original, but with the references one can do nothing. They will not fuse; and from this it may be seen that we have not really shifted one foot off our safe Nonsense ground of

[1] Belle Moses in *Lewis Carroll in Wonderland and at Home* quotes him as saying of his Nonsense language, 'A perfectly balanced mind could understand it.' (Ch. I, p. 6).

one and one and one. Pebbles, poodles, bobbles and wabbles are as good a Nonsense series as any another, and quite as intractable to the fusing powers of the dream. Provided that enough words are called up by a Nonsense neologism and provided that the references are sufficiently incompatible, Nonsense is as safe in this part of the game as in any other.

In the same way it is interesting to note that what I have called the technical terms, where no immediate chorus of connected words springs to the mind, are frequently doubled on themselves, as if to make up for their absence of evocation by creating inside themselves a tiny alliterative, rhyming or repetitive series of their own. *Jabberwocky* produces the *Jubjub*, '*Callooh! Callay!*', *snicker-snack*; Lear has *Soffsky-Poffsky*, *Clangle-Wangle*, *Boss-Woss*. They go as the vorpal sword went, one two, one two, and we are still safe inside the world of numbers and series. The same principle holds good in the Nonsense manœuvre of transplanting words from their normal context. There is only one example of this in Carroll, in the Snark:—

> As the man they called 'Ho!' told his story of woe
> In an antediluvian tone.

but Lear has a number, 'You luminous person of Barnes', 'That incipient old man at a casement', 'That intrinsic old man of Peru', and many more both in his Nonsense and his letters. The words have meanings but the mind is unable to fit the meanings, as assembled, together, and the effect once again is that of one and one and one.

That effect, however, is extremely important; it is vital that the effect should be one and one, and not nothing. So far we have been looking only at one side of the question, one half of the balancing process. We have seen how the Nonsense words, by the usual Nonsense methods, play against the mind's tendency to oneness, the tendency towards poetry and dream; but they have equally to make sure that the Nonsense words do not create a nothingness in the mind. Either form of infinity is dangerous to Nonsense, and it is between the two, between o and 1 as it were, that Nonsense language has to maintain its balance.

Nonsense has a fear of nothingness quite as great as its fear of everythingness. Mr. Empson says in *Some Versions of the Pastoral* that the fear of death is one of the crucial topics of the Alices (p. 291), but it will be simpler for us at present to think of it as a fear of nothingness.

> . . . 'for it might end, you know,' said Alice to herself, 'in my going out altogether, like a candle. I wonder what I should be like then?'
>
> (*Down the Rabbit-Hole*, A.A.W.)
>
> 'You know very well you're not real.'
> 'I *am* real!' said Alice, and began to cry.
>
> (*Tweedledum and Tweedledee*, T.L.G.)

The Snark breaks the rules here, for in Fit the Seventh someone has 'softly and suddenly vanished away', that is, has become nothingness. Nonsense does not deal in any kind of physical or metaphysical nothingness, one needs to remember. It deals in words. Where these are normal and are acting normally, there cannot be a nothingness in so far as they are concerned, for words have reference to experience. 'Word implies relation to creatures' (*Summa*, Pt. I, Q. 34, Art. 4). The only way in which nothingness could set in might be by some sort of separation between words and things, by things having no words attached to them or by words without reference to things. It comes down to a question of names.

Names come in for a good deal of attention in the Alices. 'What's your name, child?' is the first remark of the Queen of Hearts to Alice. Humpty Dumpty also enquires what her name is, but makes the rather interesting remark that it is unsatisfactory because it does not mean anything. Alice questions the need for names to mean anything, but Humpty insists on the point, as if he were trying to set up a closer connection between the name and the thing, in the case of proper nouns. Generally, we use proper nouns as pointers and nothing more. Poetry makes much use of this, using them where possible as series of lovely sounds but not entirely devoid of reference or at least of connections, since they have associational power if not much in the way of content. The content is not enough to distract the mind from the succession of sounds, but the associations will prevent the complaint that the poet is talking gibberish:—

> And all who since, baptized or infidel,
> Jousted in Aspramont or Montalban,
> Damasco, or Marocco or Trebisond,
> Or whom Biseita sent from Afric shore
> When Charlemain and all his peerage fell
> At Fontarabia. . . .
>
> (MILTON)

None the less it is noticeable that when poetry does this, it very often intersperses the proper nouns with names of things, as if to feed the mind adequately with creatures, lest it be lulled by music, a way of working which is only partially appropriate to poetry.

> Saîl of Claustra, Aelis, Azalais,
> Raimona, Tibors, Berangerë,
> 'Neath the dark gleam of the sky;
> Under night, the peacock-throated,
> Bring the saffron-coloured shell. . . .
> Mirals, Cembelins, Audiarda,
>   Remember this fire.
> Elain, Tireis, Alcmena,
> 'Mid the silver rustling of wheat. . . .
>
> (EZRA POUND)

The men of Arvad with thine army were upon thy walls round about, and the Gammadims were in thy towers . . . Syria . . . occupied in thy fairs with emeralds, purple, and broidered work, and fine linen, and coral, and agate. Judah, and the land of Israel . . . traded in thy market wheat of Minnith, and Pannag, and honey, and oil, and balm.

> Damascus was thy merchant . . . for the multitude of all
> riches; in the wine of Helbon, and white wool. Dan also
> and Javan going to and fro occupied in thy fairs: bright
> iron, cassia, and calamus were in thy market. . . .
>
> (From EZEKIEL. xxvii)

Nonsense, as we have seen, eschews beauty, but its proper nouns work in the same way as these, though the associations are verbal, the isles of Boshen recalling the Biblical land of Goshen, Chankly Bore seeming a metamorphosis of Branksome Chine, Tinniskoop of Tinnevelly and so on. The names in Nonsense are not nothingnesses; they work by association, as the names in poetry do, but their associations are with words. Here, too, in its own way, Nonsense preserves the connection between these names and things, and we are given details:—

> Landing at eve near the Zemmery Fidd
> Where the Oblong Oysters grow.
>
> (*The Dong with a Luminous Nose*, L.L.)

> . . . the Soffsky-Poffsky trees,—which were . . . covered
> with blue leaves . . .
>
> (*The Seven Families*, N.S.B.)

Of the Jubjub:—

> Its flavour when cooked is more exquisite far
> Than mutton, or oysters, or eggs:
> (Some think it keeps best in an ivory jar,
> And some, in mahogany kegs).
>
> (H.S.)

Nothingness in all these cases is successfully defeated by the number of the verbal reminiscences called up by the Nonsense words, by their close association with things, and by illustrations. The Jabberwock is pictured for us, and so are the Pobble and the Dong and the Jumblies and nearly all of Lear's inventions. The Nonsense words are sufficiently protected from nothingness; but what happens if the reverse process takes place, and things are separated from words in some way, becoming nameless?

It is interesting that such a case is dealt with explicitly in *Through the Looking-Glass*, in Alice's entry into the wood where things have no name. This is at the end of Chapter III, *Looking-Glass Insects*, a very significant chapter despite its rather limited title, for it is all about words and names. It starts with Alice trying to make a survey of the country and attempting to name, as one might do in geography, the mountains and rivers and towns. Then comes the scene in the railway carriage which we have already discussed with reference to the remark, 'Language is worth a thousand pounds a word!' Soon after this, two remarks are made to Alice about knowing her own name and knowing the alphabet, and then begins a series of puns, made by the Gnat. It is as if, having got words and references put together at this point (as they were not at the beginning of the chapter, where Alice says, 'Principal mountains—I'm on the only one, but I don't think it's got any name') and having realized the value of it—worth a thousand pounds a word—one can start playing with it. Puns, as we have seen, are a safe enough game for Nonsense, because they are real portmanteaux, where the two meanings are distinct but are incongruously connected by an accident of language formation. After the puns, Alice and the Gnat discuss the purpose of names, and whether they have any use. Then follows another game with words: Alice's horse-fly becomes a rockinghorse-fly, the butterfly a bread-and-butter-fly. A piece of each word is allowed to develop, rather as Lear's people develop enormous noses, all out of proportion. Images in Nonsense are not allowed to develop, to turn into or mingle with other images as happens in dreams and poetry; but words may do so, provided they merely develop into another word, and by their development accentuate an incongruity. Here again, circumstantial details are given at once: 'Its wings are thin slices of bread-and-butter, its body is a crust, and its head is a lump of sugar.' Looking-Glass Insects, in fact, are not insects at all but compounds of words to which are added lists of properties in the best Nonsense manner.

The next stage is a further discussion on names. 'I suppose you don't want to lose your name? . . . only think how convenient it would be if you could manage to go home without it!' Alice is a little nervous about such an idea, and the Wood where things have no names, to which she proceeds immediately after this conversation, is frighteningly dark. Once in it, she cannot remember her own name or give a name to any of the objects round her. This is a terrifying situation, but Carroll preserves the reader from it by subjecting Alice alone to the experiment; the passage in the book makes no attempt to forgo the use of names. It is at this point that Alice meets the Fawn, a pretty creature 'with its large gentle eyes . . . Such a sweet soft voice it had!' It asks her name, and she makes a similar enquiry, but neither can remember, and they proceed lovingly—the word is Carroll's own—till they emerge from the wood. There each remembers its name and identity, and in a flash they are parted.

This passage is one of the most interesting in the Alices. There is a suggestion here that to lose your name is to gain freedom in some way, since the nameless one would no longer be under control: 'There wouldn't be any name for her to call, and of course you wouldn't have to go, you know.' It also suggests that the loss of language brings with it an increase in loving unity with living things. It is words that separate the fawn and the child, just as they separate the Yonghy-Bonghy-Bò and his love in that wood of Bong-trees where we began:—

> 'Though you're such a Hoddy Doddy,
> 'Yet I wish that I could modi-
>   'fy the words I needs must say!
>   'Will you please to go away?'

Nonsense is a game with words. Its own inventions wander safely between the respective pitfalls of 0 and 1, nothingness and everythingness; but where words without things are safe enough, things without words are far more dangerous. To have no name is to be a kind of nothing:—

> 'What do you call yourself?' the Fawn said . . .
> She answered rather sadly, 'Nothing just now.'

But it is also to have unexpected opportunities for unity and that is a step towards everythingness. We are safe with *brillig* and the *Jabberwock* because that is a fight, a dialectic and an equilibrium; but despite the Yonghy-Bonghy-Bò and the Bong-trees—words which as we have seen play the Nonsense game in the usual way—and despite the early pumpkins and the jug without a handle, something has crept in here which words cannot cover, cannot split up and control. There is a nostalgia in each of these scenes:—

> Alice stood looking after it, almost ready to cry with vexation at having lost her dear little fellow-traveller so suddenly.

> On that coast of Coromandel,
> In his jug without a handle
>   Still she weeps, and daily moans;
>   On that little heap of stones
>   To her Dorking hens she moans . . .

But Nonsense can admit of no emotion—that gate to everythingness and nothingness where ultimately words fail completely. It is a game, to which emotion is alien, and it will allow none to its playthings, which are words and those wielders of words, human beings. Its humans, like its words and things and Nonsense vocabulary, have to be one, and one, and one. There is nothing more inexorable than a game.

Chapter 11

CUNNING OLD FURY

T HERE IS still one group of words left which we have
to examine, to see what Nonsense does with them.
These are what I have called, very generally, abstracts,
words where a certain familiar collection of letters and
sounds, T R U T H perhaps, or G L O R Y, or L O V E, covers a
multitude of rather vague and personal notions, with no
very close correspondence between mind and mind as
regards the definition of the term. Reference here does not
take kindly to precise definition, i.e. to limitation. The
minds which use these words are not generally aware of
this lack of limitation and of precise communicative power;
the words are used quite freely in ordinary life, their aura
of associations being sometimes recognized as such, but
more often mistaken for a reference, a feeling being substituted for an intellectual content. In consequence the
mind when using or receiving such words tends to be more
passive than active, to be worked upon by the words
rather than in control of them. The disorder side of the
mind has rather too much play here, and the mind passes
into the control of its own equipment, as happens in
dreams also.

This brand of word has been termed 'emotive' by certain writers on the subject, an unpleasant term but one
which at least shows that these words produce movement,
a moving of the feelings rather than an effect on the intellect. The word 'emotion' brings with it the idea of movement, just as the word 'passion' by virtue of its derivation
implies the suffering of something, a state of passivity. St.
Thomas gives a list of eleven passions, useful in showing
that the term is not to be interpreted too narrowly: love,
hatred, joy, sorrow, desire, aversion, daring, fear, hope,

despair, anger. In either case, whether we think of ourselves as moved by emotion or suffering passion, we are
controlled rather than controlling, are played with rather
than playing our own game.

In Nonsense, as we have seen, the intellect must be in
control of its material. In theory, therefore, the mind in
the Nonsense universe, be it the mind of the maker or the
guest, must not be acted upon by any of the emotive words
that may be employed. This is sound sporting practice. In
a game one must not lose one's temper, get in a panic, love
or hate one's fellow-players, experience affection or revulsion in connection with one's playthings. (I remember
as a child having so particular an affection for the Knave
of Hearts in a pack of cards that I could never bear to play
him out of my hand, with dire results on the game.) The
only feeling appropriate to a game, in fact essential to it,
is a love of power and a desire to win. 'It is naturally
pleasant to overcome, inasmuch as it makes a man to appre-
ciate his own superiority. Wherefore all those games in
which there is a striving for the mastery, and a possibility
of winning it, afford the greatest pleasure' (*Summa*, Pt.
I—II, Q. 32, Art. 6). So, too, Alice says, 'I don't want to
be anybody's prisoner. I want to be a Queen' ('*It's My
Own Invention*', T.L.G.)

Provided the player can maintain his independence,
however, he can play with these words as with any others,
though perhaps with a few additional safeguards. Nonsense will not exclude them just because they are potentially dangerous material with their leaning towards
irrationality. Nonsense is supremely concerned with the
rational mind. Emotion and passion are to be thought of
as a separate department from this; but for all that, the
individual possessing both is a unity, and it is interesting
that whereas the numbering and logical and orderly side
of the mind has little to do with emotion, dreams have a
great deal, so that if we are to ally passion and emotion
with one side or the other of the mind, it will inevitably

be the dream and disorder side, which Nonsense plays against. Dreams more often than not generate intense and varied emotions in the dreamer. In view of this alliance, Nonsense will do what it has done before in similar circumstances—use material apparently suitable to dream and disorder so as to engage that side of the mind in play, but inhibit its development in some way. We have already considered how this works in the case of images. There Nonsense prevents the formation of trains of association or the identification of one image with another, or of the mind with them. Here, with emotive words, it will have to prevent the development of trains of feeling and the identification of the self with the feelings described or conjured up. Passion and emotion will be human qualities like any other. The Old Person of Bangor, 'Whose face was distorted with anger', will take his place alongside the Old Man of Melrose, 'Who walked on the tips of his toes', and on exactly the same matter-of-fact level.

Nonsense sets about its task in characteristic fashion. Feelings, by their nature, do not fit very well into words, and are more concerned with people than things. This is exactly contrary to the nature of Nonsense, which will accordingly treat matters of emotion according to its own rules, emphasizing words rather than their supposed content, the verbal rather than the real, and will keep as close to things as possible. Poetry also employs things in connection with abstracts, emotions and passions, but with a different aim in view, using beautiful things to enhance the feeling of attraction, perhaps of identification, in the mind, or repulsive or frightening things to set up a stronger reaction of withdrawal. In either case the mind is being played with, subjected to the images, brought into that passion or passivity which is half of poetry's way of working, inducing in the mind a consent to being played with.

When will you ever, Peace, wild wooddove, shy wings shut,

Your roaming round me end, and under be my
  boughs?

(HOPKINS)

And Joy whose hand is ever at his lips
Bidding adieu; and aching Pleasure nigh,
Turning to poison while the bee-mouth sips.

(KEATS)

Now what is Love I will thee tell:
It is the fountain and the well
Where Pleasure and Repentance dwell.

(THOMAS HEYWOOD)

Fear at my heart, as at a cup,
My lifeblood seemed to sip.

(COLERIDGE)

And through each brain, on hands of pain,
Another's terror crept.

(OSCAR WILDE)

Nonsense must work differently. It too will surround its
abstracts with things, but things like bats and tea-trays,
to which the mind feels complete indifference. It will also,
where possible, turn its people into things or at least into
playthings alongside its other playthings for which the
mind feels neither attraction nor the contrary.

We can look first at the emphasis on words rather than
on feeling or reality. The constant cry of the Queen of
Hearts, 'Off with his head!' is in the end reduced to a
mere expression by the Gryphon—'It's all her fancy that:
they never executes nobody, you know.' The sorrow of the
Mock Turtle, 'sighing as if his heart would break', is dealt
with in the same way. 'It's all his fancy, that: he hasn't
got no sorrow, you know.' Instead of grounds for grief we
get a history, told with a greater concentration of puns
(a linguistic rather than meaningful artifice) than anywhere else in the Alices. Fear is turned into an inability
to remember one's own name, as with the White Queen
at the end of the *Looking-Glass*. The tiger-lily in *The
Garden of Live Flowers* is thrown into a passion by words,

'When one speaks, they all begin together, and it's enough to make one wither to hear the way they go on.' It is soothed, however, by a compliment, i.e. more words. Alice has resort to a long word, said aloud, as comfort after the very abrupt ending of her interview with Humpty Dumpty. The word G L O R Y in Humpty Dumpty's mouth is reduced to meaning 'There's a nice knock-down argument for you!', a matter of verbal dialectic and nothing more. In certain cases we are deflected from emotion to the actual writing or spelling of the words themselves, a sort of extension of the game, 'I love my love with an H'.

> 'Give your evidence,' the King repeated angrily, 'or I'll have you executed, whether you are nervous or not.'
>
> .   .   .   .   .   .
>
> 'The twinkling of *what*?' said the King.
> 'It *began* with the tea,' the Hatter replied.
> 'Of course twinkling *begins* with a T!' said the King.
>
> (*Who Stole The Tarts?*, A.A.W.)

The next is a perfect example of this manœuvre:—

> 'There's the White Queen running across the country! She came flying out of the wood over yonder—How fast those Queens *can* run!'
> 'There's some enemy after her, no doubt,' the King said, without even looking round. 'That wood's full of them.'
> 'But aren't you going to run and help her?' Alice asked, very much surprised at his taking it so quietly.
> 'No use, no use!' said the King. 'She runs so fearfully quick. You might as well try to catch a Bandersnatch! But I'll make a memorandum about her, if you like—— She's a dear good creature,' he repeated softly to himself, as he opened his memorandum-book. 'Do you spell "creature" with a double "e"?'
>
> (*The Lion and the Unicorn*, T.L.G.)

There is another rather similar case earlier in the *Looking-Glass*, in Chapter I:—

'The horror of that moment,' the King went on, 'I shall never, *never* forget!'

'You will, though,' the Queen said, 'if you don't make a memorandum of it.'

Alice looked on with great interest as the King took an enormous memorandum-book out of his pocket, and began writing.

In this instance, however, we are still further safeguarded, just as there is a Nonsense word introduced in the last one, the Bandersnatch, to keep us on the right lines. Here Alice moves the pencil for the King and does his writing for him; and we are shifted immediately into the realm of observation of things.

'What manner of things?' said the Queen, looking over the book (in which Alice had put '*The White Knight is sliding down the poker. He balances very badly.*'). 'That's not a memorandum of *your* feelings!'

These forms of insulation against emotion and dream—the emphasis on words, the introduction of Nonsense vocabulary, the directing of the attention to things—may occur in conjunction as well as separately; take the following example, where a thing—a beaver to which, like a bat, we are indifferent—a Nonsense word and the series of numbers all tie down the idea of emotion:—

> The Beaver had counted with scrupulous care,
>> Attending to every word:
> But it fairly lost heart, and outgrabe in despair,
>> When the third repetition occurred.
>>>> (Fit the Fifth, H.S.)

Sometimes the word may be negatived outright, by a deliberate contradiction.

''Tis so,' said the Duchess: 'and the moral of that is—"Oh, 'tis love, 'tis love, that makes the world go round!"'

'Somebody said,' Alice whispered, 'that it's done by everybody minding their own business!'

K

'Ah well! It means much the same thing,' said the Duchess. . . .

> (*The Mock Turtle's Story*, A.A.W.)

. . . they pursued their voyage with the utmost delight and apathy.

. . . the whole party from the boat was gazing at him with mingled affection and disgust. . . .

> (*The Four Little Children*, N.S.B.)

. . . they gave a tea-party and a garden-party and a ball, and a concert, and then returned to their respective homes full of joy and respect, sympathy, satisfaction, and disgust.

> (*The Seven Families*, N.S.B.)

The most constant of the Nonsense rules for dealing with this type of word, however, is to surround it with words referring to things, and to those things with which Nonsense prefers to play. The aim, in part at least, is to distract the mind's attention from the vagueness of the emotion or the qualities of temperament named to something concrete and manageable:—

'Maybe it's always pepper that makes people hot-tempered,' she went on, very much pleased at having found out a new kind of rule, 'and vinegar that makes them sour—and camomile that makes them bitter—and—and barley-sugar and such things that make children sweet-tempered.'

> (*The Mock Turtle's Story*, A.A.W.)

So whenever an abstract occurs, particularly if it is one connected with the feelings in some way, it is frequently tethered down by a thing, and a completely unromantic and matter-of-fact thing, beside it.

They sought it with thimbles, they sought it with care;
They pursued it with forks and hope;

> (H.S.)

'A little kindness—and putting her hair in papers—would do wonders with her——'

> (*Queen Alice*, T.L.G.)

There was an old man whose remorse,
Induced him to drink Caper Sauce;

There was an Old Man at a Junction,
Whose feelings were wrung with compunction;
When they said 'The Train's gone!' He exclaimed
  'How forlorn!'
But remained on the rails of the Junction.

There was an old man whose despair
Induced him to purchase a hare;

(M.N.)

Lear in any case treats the emotions and passions with considerable reserve in his limericks:—

There was an old person of Pett,
Who was partly consumed by regret;
He sate in a cart, and ate cold apple tart,
Which relieved that old person of Pett.

There was an old person of Newry,
Whose manners were tinctured with fury;
He tore all the rugs, and broke all the jugs
Within twenty miles' distance of Newry.

There was an old person in gray,
Whose feelings were tinged with dismay;
She purchased two parrots, and fed them on carrots,
Which pleased that old person in gray.

(M.N.)

With the addition of this delicacy of touch, Lear follows the regular Nonsense pattern, and we are turned from emotion to things in each case.

That brings us to the next point, for it is one of the characteristics of Nonsense that people tend to be turned into things also, not in the sense of magic, where a frog becomes a Prince, but in the sense of being turned into playthings. People are not excluded from the Nonsense game—(though it has a tendency to whittle down their humanity, to make them chessmen rather than men, court cards rather than a real court, madmen like the Hatter, or imaginary half-human beings like the Pobble, the Dong and the Yonghy-Bonghy-Bò). The playthings of Nonsense are words, and too many words to be left out have reference to human life and behaviour, quite apart from the fact that the whole game takes place inside a human mind with a life and behaviour of its own. Games in any case borrow the term 'men' for the objects of play. Chess, halma and draughts are all played with 'men', and every pack of cards has twelve picture cards—pictures of people—added to the numerical ones. None the less, these are playthings just as much as bats and balls and counters. They are in the power of the player who is free to treat them exactly as he pleases, within the rules of the game, and the people who occur in Nonsense have to abide by this same rule. A game requires a certain ruthlessness of its own, both as regards objects of play and opponents, within clearly defined limits—hence the notion of the 'foul'. It is as the White Knight says to the Red before they fight:—'You will observe the Rules of Battle, of course?' to which the other replies, 'I always do.' But they are Rules of Battle, and a good deal of rough treatment is involved.

This roughness applies particularly to the human body, the thing which, after all, is nearest to the emotions, and it is treated with that absence of feeling that is proper to a game, an absence of feeling on both sides, the player feeling nothing and assuming that the plaything feels nothing either. It is this that accounts for the apparent cruelty in Nonsense. To children and to the mind in play, the people have become things; no contact of feeling or sympathy with them is permissible, and so it does not matter if they meet with dreadful fates, in great variety. Lear is full of examples of this sort of thing:—

> There was an Old Man of Nepaul,
> From his horse had a terrible fall;
> But, though split quite in two, by some very
>   strong glue
> They mended that Man of Nepaul.   (B.N.)

'We wish to chop you into bits to mix you into Stuffin'!'
(*The Two Old Bachelors*, L.L.)

Nursery Rhyme has this same robust carelessness over its objects:—

> I took him by the left leg,
> And threw him down the stairs.

> The pig was eat and Tom was beat
> And Tom went roaring down the street.

> The barber shaved the mason.
>   As I suppose,
>   Cut off his nose
> And popped it in a bason.

> There was a Man of Thessaly,
> And he was wondrous wise:
> He jumped into a quickset hedge
> And scratched out both his eyes;
> But when he saw his eyes were out,
> With all his might and main
> He jumped into another hedge
> And scratched them in again.

> Fee fi fo fum!
> I smell the blood of an Englishman!
> Be he alive or be he dead,
> I'll grind his bones to make my bread!

> There came a little blackbird
> And pecked off her nose.

Lear has an equivalent of that last example, but takes the matter one stage further into Nonsense by bringing us back to words again:—

> There was an old man of Dunrose;
> A parrot seized hold of his nose.
> When he grew melancholy, They said, 'His
>   name's Polly',
> Which soothed that old man of Dunrose.

(M.N.)

It is this treating of people as things which lies behind the Ruthless Rhymes of the kind: 'Hush, hush, my dear, that is Papa, Run over by a tram.' Lear's people provide numerous rounds of the game. They are eaten by wild beasts—The young lady of Clare; drowned—The old persons of Ems and Cadiz; squashed flat—The Young Lady of Norway; die of a surfeit of muffins—The Old Man of Calcutta; are smashed with a hammer—The Old Person of Buda; their noses are burnt off—the Odious Little Boy in *The Four Little Children*; they are 'scrunched with a stick', a very graphic description of the activities of the death-dealing Old Lady of Stroud. It is alarmingly like Saint Paul's catalogue of the fates of the Early Christians in the Epistle to the Hebrews. But the victims accept their fate with magnificent sang-froid, as the reader may do also. The Pobble is a little sorry at having lost his toes 'in a manner so far from pleasant', but is consoled by a feed. Lear's old man who suffers grievous bodily injury is merely a little put out:—

> There was an old Person of Chester,
> Whom several small children did pester;
> They threw some large stones, which broke
>   most of his bones,
> And displeased that old person of Chester. (B.N.)

This is like the White Knight's attitude to a similar calamity:—

> She was quite frightened this time, and said in an anxious tone, as she picked him up, 'I hope no bones are broken?'
> 'None to speak of,' the Knight said, . . .
>   ('*It's My Own Invention*', T.L.G.)

Lear's characters are equally imperturbable:—

> There was an Old Man of the Nile,
> Who sharpened his nails with a file;
> Till he cut off his thumbs, and said calmly,
>   'This comes—
> Of sharpening one's nails with a file!'

There was an Old Person of Tartary,
Who divided his jugular artery;
But he screeched to his wife, and she said,
  'Oh, my life!
Your death will be felt by all Tartary!'

This is classic Nonsense, the *haute école*. The detachment
of those involved is perfect; but in the last case there is the
wife's detachment as well as the victim's, and that is an important point, for if people are things in the Nonsense
game, they must, when they meet, treat one another as
such, and this involves detachment from any form of affection or kindliness. Relationships between them will be
matter-of-fact but not matter for feeling. People have to
be kept separate from one another, so that they will be
as much one and one and one as the rest of the Nonsense
world. Next of kin may be nearest but must most certainly
not be dearest. In the last example, and in the Lewis
Carroll one given earlier where the White King refuses
to go to his wife's rescue, we see what happens to the
husband-and-wife relationship in Nonsense. There are
other examples:—

There was an Old Man on some rocks,
Who shut up his wife in a box,
When she said, 'Let me out,' he exclaimed,
  'Without doubt,
You will pass all your life in that box.'

There was an Old Man of Peru,
Who watched his wife making a stew;
But once by mistake, in a stove she did bake,
That unfortunate Man of Peru.

(B.N.)

If anyone is inclined to take that 'by mistake' too seriously,
they have only to look at the picture accompanying the
rhyme. Nursery rhyme can produce the same kind of
thing:—

Nebuchadnezzar, the King of the Jews,
Sold his wife for a pair of shoes . . .

The same dissolution has occurred in the parent-child relationship. Here are examples of parents' attitude to their offspring:—

> 'Speak roughly to your little boy,
> And beat him when he sneezes' . . .

While the Duchess sang the second verse of the song, she kept tossing the baby violently up and down, and the poor little thing howled so, that Alice could hardly hear the words. . . .
'Here! You may nurse it a bit, if you like!' the Duchess said to Alice, flinging the baby at her as she spoke.

> (*Pig and Pepper*, A.A.W.)

'Be off, or I'll kick you downstairs!'
> (Father William to his son,
> *Advice from a Caterpillar*, A.A.W.)

> There was an old person of Pisa,
> Whose daughters did nothing to please her;
> She dressed them in gray, and banged them
>   all day,
> Round the walls of the city of Pisa.
>
> (M.N.)

> There was a Young Person of Smyrna,
> Whose Grandmother threatened to burn her;
> But she seized on the cat, and said, 'Granny,
>   burn that!
> You incongruous Old Woman of Smyrna'.

> The tiger on the other hand is kittenish and mild;
> He makes a pleasant playfellow for any little child.
> And mothers of large families who live by commonsense,
> Will find a tiger well repay the trouble and expense.
>
> (BELLOC)

Mr. Discobbolos goes one better, and blows up the whole of his family with a charge of dynamite:—

> And all the Discobbolos family flew
> In thousands of bits to the sky so blue.
>
> (L.L.)

The children respond in kind:—

> 'Hold your tongue, Ma!' said the young Crab, a trifle snappishly. 'You're enough to try the patience of an oyster!'
>
> (*A Caucus-Race and a Long Tale*, A.A.W.)

> There was an Old Man of the East,
> Who gave all his children a feast;
> But they all ate so much, and their conduct was such,
> That it killed that Old Man of the East.
>
> (B.N.)

> I won't be my Father's Jack . . .
> I won't be my Mother's Jill . . .

It is not merely from one's relations that one is isolated, though it is obvious that Nonsense would make a dead set at them, since its structure requires as few relations, in a slightly different but congruous sense, as possible. The same thing happens, however, with everyone with whom Nonsense is concerned. Alice is continually treated as a thing without feeling by the creatures she encounters. The flowers regard her as one of them rather than a sentient human: 'You're beginning to fade, you know—and then one ca'n't help one's petals getting a little untidy.' So does the pudding: 'I wonder how you'd like it if I were to cut a slice out of *you*, you creature!' The gratuitous and recurring rudeness and refusal to co-operate of practically every being she meets are all part of the insulation of one from another. Not one individual is kind to the child the whole way through both stories, with the possible exception of the White Knight, who at least is not unkind; but as for the others:—

> 'You!' said the Caterpillar contemptuously. 'Who are you?'
>
> (*Advice from a Caterpillar*, A.A.W.)

> 'But what am *I* to do?' said Alice.
> 'Anything you like,' said the Footman, and began whistling.
>
> (*Pig and Pepper*, A.A.W.)

'But it may rain *outside?*'

'It may—if it chooses,' said Tweedledee: 'we've no objection.'

'Selfish things!' thought Alice. . . .

(Tweedledum and Tweedledee, T.L.G.)

Just then the door opened a little way, and a creature with a long beak put its head out for a moment and said, 'No admittance till the week after next!' and shut the door again with a bang.

(Queen Alice, T.L.G.)

The absence of sympathy and fellow-feeling is fundamental. In Lear it has its embodiment in the 'they' of the limericks:—

There was an Old Man with a beard,
Who sat on a horse when he reared;
But they said, 'Never mind! you will fall off
    behind!
You propitious Old Man with a beard!'

There was an old man who screamed out
Whenever they knocked him about;
So they took off his boots, and fed him with
    fruits,
And continued to knock him about.

(M.N.)

The force of that final 'And' is remarkable.

This absence of relationships, other than those required and controlled by the processes of the game, means not merely that each individual is separate from every other, but that the mind of the player is isolated as well, within the framework of the game. This, I believe, is the true purpose of the dream which ushers in each of the Alices. It is not to induce a dreaming state of mind as such, with its tangle of associations and its irrationality. It is to isolate the mind completely from all possible contact with real life and real people, with which games have nothing to do. No-one is more isolated than the dreamer, unless it be the lunatic, of whom there may be more to say later. This sense of isolation is a feature of Nonsense. It is the logical conclusion of the methods and operations we have observed, and is implicit in the aim of any player—to win, to become a Queen, 'because there never was more than one Queen at a time' (T.L.G.). Only one being or one side can win, and the fact that at the end of the Caucus-race the announcement is made: 'All have won and all must have prizes' makes it clear that the race was not a race at all.

The sense of isolation is perhaps the one emotion permissible in Nonsense, since it emphasizes the unattached nature of the player, and so contributes to one of the main principles of the game itself. It may take the form of a boast:—

> I'm the King of the Castle.
> Get down, you dirty rascal.

It may be a statement, even a statement of the obvious:—

> Here come I:
> Little Jumping Joan.
> When nobody's with me
> I'm always alone.

'Why do you sit out here all alone?' said Alice, not wishing to start an argument.

'Why, because there's nobody with me!' cried Humpty Dumpty.

(T.L.G.)

But even in Nursery Rhyme the note of awareness of solitude creeps in:—

> The other flew after,
> And then there was none:
> And so the poor stone
> Was left all alone.

On three occasions in the Alices, the heroine bursts into tears, complaining, 'I am so *very* lonely.' Lear is full of it, from the chorus of *Calico Pie*, 'They never came back to me', to the Pelican Chorus:—

> She has gone to the great Gromboolian plain,
> And we probably never shall meet again!

to the abandoned Dong, the forsaken Yonghy-Bonghy-Bò, and the Quangle-Wangle who complains:—

> But the longer I live on this Crumpetty Tree
> The plainer than ever it seems to me
> That very few people come this way,
> And life on the whole is far from gay.

If this were just an awareness of isolation all would be well, for that, if it were unemotional and detached, might fit very well into the Nonsense game. Plenty of Lear's people in the limericks are in comparative or in total isolation, and this is all part of the game, as with the Old Person of Spain who cut himself off from trouble and pain by sitting on a chair with his feet in the air, or Mr. and Mrs. Discobbolos who take refuge in isolation on the top of a wall. It is clear, however, that in Lear's Nonsense songs at least something else has got in, and that is pain. Alice's expressions of it and her tears leave us unmoved, as they should do. It is just another turn of play, and the White Queen directs Alice's, and our, attention back where it belongs, to the exercise of the intellect rather than that of the feelings: 'Consider what a great girl you are. Consider what a long way you've come today. Consider what o'clock it is. Consider anything, only don't cry!' Alice is sceptical about this method of dealing with emotion, saying, 'Can *you* keep from crying by considering things?' and gets the categorical answer, 'That's the way it's done.' With Lear, however, the insulation does not altogether work. There is a genuine pathos in the Dong and the Yonghy-Bonghy-Bò, even in some odd way in the Jumblies, and I remember disliking that song when I was a child for that reason, resenting the intrusion into the game of an adult and alien emotion. The limericks are pure Nonsense and have nothing of this quality of feeling about them; but in the Songs one feels that Lear is, quite literally, not playing the game. They are rather more or rather less than Nonsense, and in consequence the game ceases to be a game and becomes something else.

It is interesting that something similar, though different in its effects, happens with *The Hunting of the Snark*. This work has always lagged behind the Alices in popularity, undeservedly, so some critics say; but it is noticeable that it produces on the reader, not the intellectual delight of the other two books, but something nearer emotion, though of a shadowy kind, a slight sensation of distaste and disquiet, and the *Sylvie and Bruno* books multiply this ten times over.

The Songs and the Snark are, strictly speaking, failures as Nonsense. They upset the game, but the nature of the upsetting is interesting, for in each case it has to do with emotion. Lear allows emotion into his Songs, and so turns them into something else, something that is very near poetry. Carroll never comes within a thousand miles of poetry; instead, we have in the Snark something which, quite frankly, feels a little mad, the result of trying to play with everything on one's own terms, suffering nothing but controlling everything.

> 'I'll be judge, I'll be jury,'
> Said cunning old Fury;
> 'I'll try the whole cause
> And condemn you to death.'

Those strange verses which occur early in Wonderland seem to have no point at all beyond their typographical arrangement. But this theme, of exercising oneself all the functions in a Court of Law is caught up again in the Snark, Fit the Sixth, where the Snark is at one and the same time Counsel for the Defence, the Judge who sums up and passes sentence, and the Jury who consider the verdict. In fact Old Fury and the Snark respectively fulfil all the offices except that of prisoner. 'I don't want to be anybody's prisoner,' as Alice remarked; but in that case you have to go on playing your own game for ever and ever, so as to keep the initiative in your own hands.

Nonsense like any other game needs to end somewhere. The time of any game is limited, and the player has to be ready and willing to return to real life afterwards. The only two Lear limericks which are at all alarming are, curiously enough, two which carry with them a suggestion of eternity:—

> There is a Young Lady whose nose
> Continually prospers and grows.
> When it grew out of sight, she exclaimed in
>   a fright,
> 'O! Goodbye to the end of my nose!'

That is the only limerick which is in the present tense.

> There was an Old Man who said, 'Well!
> Will *nobody* answer this bell?
> I have pulled day and night, till my hair has
>   turned white,
> But nobody answers this bell!'

The Alices end with a return to reality; the Four Little Children complete their voyage round the world, and the Seven Families of the Lake Pipple-Popple are wound up and disposed of in seven glass bottles—indeed each chapter of this story has its own ending, 'And that was the end of the Seven young Geese', and so on. But the Snark is much more indefinite, with its soft, sudden vanishing away, and so are the Nonsense songs where the Dong roams for ever, lighted by his nose, the Daddy Long-Legs and Fly play at battlecock and shuttledore, and the Lady Jingly Jones weeps to her hens. As for *Sylvie and Bruno Concluded*, it is not concluded at all. Something has gone off the rails here, and we must try in the next chapter to discover what it is.

Chapter 12

'THE HEART IS AFFECTED'

WE COME now to what I have called the Nonsense failures—in Lear's case the Nonsense songs such as the Dong and the Jumblies, and in Carroll's the Snark and the two halves of *Sylvie and Bruno*. They are to be regarded technically as failures because in them the separation between player and material is beginning to fail, and the term 'player' here will include both Nonsense writer and Nonsense reader. If the game is to continue uninhibited, the mind of the player, Lear's or Carroll's or our own, must not get drawn into its own game or become identified with it. Detachment is necessary for control. When the Nonsense writer is detached and in control of his own material, our play goes along beautifully; but the minute he loses his detachment we also become implicated, and the atmosphere changes at once, generating emotion or a sense of the reality and earnestness of what is going on instead of that state of security, freedom and purely mental delight which is proper to the game. We are acted upon instead of acting.

From this it follows, partly, that these particular Nonsense productions are failures because too much of their creators can be found in them, and in consequence this stage of the enquiry will be rather less clearly defined than was the case up till now. People and emotions have got into the game, or at least on to the playing field, and they are not analysable into tidy parts or neat chapters. We can only make suggestions, realizing as we go along that our own minds are not here very clearly differentiated from our subject-matter, for where Lear and Carroll become involved in their own game, so do we. Our curls get entangled together like those of the Frog and Fish

149

Footmen, and we have to be patient with them and ourselves.

We can begin with *The Hunting of the Snark*. This was published four years after *Through the Looking-Glass* and thirteen years before *Sylvie and Bruno*. One would hesitate to class the two *Sylvie and Bruno* books as Nonsense, were it not that in the Preface to the first Carroll hopes it may prove 'acceptable nonsense'. In the same preface he admits that he was here attempting to strike a completely new note; but he had no such intention in writing the *Snark*. In a rhyming letter sent with the book to a little girl, we find Old Father William and the Snark hobnobbing, as if they could agree very well together, and much of the Nonsense vocabulary of *Jabberwocky* reappears in the Snark. It is presumably meant to produce the same effect. In the Preface to this work, Carroll congratulates himself upon its status as Nonsense: '*If*—and the thing is wildly possible—the charge of writing nonsense were ever brought against the author of this brief but instructive poem . . .' The effect the Snark does in fact produce is completely different from that of the Alices. We need not look for any psychological reasons for this. We can maintain our procedure of considering Nonsense as a game; we have worked out by now a general idea of its rules—and the Snark breaks practically every one.

There was to be in Nonsense nothing vague, shadowy or imprecise, no dream or delirium or madness, nothing that would allow the disorder side of the mind to take over. Yet all these elements are present in the Snark:—

I engage with the Snark—every night after dark—
    In a dreamy delirious fight:
I serve it with greens in those shadowy scenes . . .
                            (Fit the Third)

He dreamed that he stood in a shadowy Court . . .
                            (Fit the Sixth)

Words whose utter inanity proved his insanity . . .
                            (Fit the Seventh)

Genuine similes are forbidden, lest some sort of dream fusion take place in the mind. But there is one here, in Fit the Third:—

> And my heart is like nothing so much as a bowl
> Brimming over with quivering curds!

The objects whose names are used should neither attract nor repel, and should not have any sort of congruity amongst themselves; but here there are certain passages where just such a thing occurs. In the phrase 'They charmed it with smiles and soap', for instance, the two entities immediately combine in the mind to suggest the unpleasant metaphorical sense of 'soft soap'. The same slightly unpleasant mixture occurs with food in one or two places. Food as such is normally attractive, but here it has got mixed with unattractive things, and the result is not detachment but a slight sense of revulsion.

> . . . you may serve it with greens,
> And it's handy for striking a light.
> (Fit the Third)
> . . . Such as 'Fry me!' or 'Fritter my wig!'
> His intimate friends called him 'Candle-ends',
> And his enemies 'Toasted Cheese.'
> (Fit the First)
> You boil it in sawdust: you salt it in glue:
> You condense it with locusts and tape.
> (Fit the Fifth)

A game depends for its progress upon a measure of free mobility; yet here contradiction is so introduced as to inhibit the mind's mobility. It is well enough at the verbal level, as in Alice's interview with the Caterpillar; and in *Looking-Glass*, Alice's apparently contradictory project of walking in the opposite direction in order to reach her destination is perfectly logical since the action takes place in a mirror. But it is better not to contradict the possibility of movement, as is done here:—

'. . . Steer to starboard, but keep her head larboard!'

L

> . . . Then the bowsprit got mixed with the rudder some-
> times. . . .
> . . . he *had* hoped, at least, when the wind blew due East,
> That the ship would not travel due West!
>
> (Fit the Second)

Carroll himself picks up the second of these three phrases
for a commentary in the Preface, as if even he saw that
all was not quite as it should be. In fact, if Nonsense is to
be logical, this is exactly the type of contradiction it
cannot afford to admit.

Nonsense must have no truck with infinity, in the form
of nothingness. Yet there are two forms of nothingness in
the Snark, a map that is 'A perfect and absolute blank',
and the vanishing of the Baker at the end of the story.
One may contrast that map of a vacuum with Lear's
precise Nonsense geography. In the soft and sudden
vanishing of one of the characters, another Nonsense rule
is broken, that which insists that language is safe and
inviolable; for he is cut off halfway through a word, and
there follows

> A weary and wandering sigh
> That sounded like '-jum' but others declare
> It was only a breeze went by.

Not only a man has vanished but a word too, and for
Nonsense that is a much more serious loss.

This vanishing is expressed as a personal terror earlier:
'And the notion I cannot endure!' Fear occurs fairly
constantly throughout.

> The Beaver turned pale to the tip of its tail,
> And even the Butcher felt queer.
>
> (Fit the Fifth)

> . . . And grabbed at the Banker, who shrieked in despair
> For he knew it was useless to fly.

> . . . Led on by that fear-stricken yell . . .
>
> (Fit the Seventh)

To add to this, the Banker is struck dumb, and language

thus receives another blow. Certain descriptions of the setting are of a frightening kind:—

> Yet at first sight the crew were not pleased with the view,
>   Which consisted of chasms and crags.
>
> (Fit the Second)

> A dismal and desolate valley.

> But the valley got narrower and narrower still,
>   And the evening got darker and colder . . .

> Then a scream, shrill and high, rent the shuddering sky

> While strange creepy creatures came out of their dens
>   And watched them with wondering eyes.
>
> (Fit the Fifth)

A whole pack of emotions is allowed in. We have tears from the Beaver (twice), from the Baker, from the Butcher (twice), from the pig's jailer; the Bellman is 'unmanned . . . with generous emotion'. In addition the Bellman registers anger, indignation, perplexity, wrath and distress; the Beaver, Butcher and Judge, disgust; even the Jub-jub 'lives in perpetual passion'.

Worst of all, there is evidence of affection between Bellman and Beaver, and later between Beaver and Butcher. Love is the most dangerous element possible for Nonsense. The reasons for this are fairly clear. First, it is supremely unitive (and Nonsense may allow no unification). It leaves no heart unmoved. At its finest, it creates in the human individual a beautiful balance between giving and receiving, action and passion. It has special affinities with poetry, and, in its wilder manifestations, with madness. It demands the subjection of the whole individual, attainting and to some extent suppressing the logical intellect. All this is anathema to Nonsense, which protects itself in various ways from this intruder into its game-world. It is curious and interesting, for instance, that Carroll should have chosen for one of the principal characters of Wonderland the Queen of Hearts. With her,

one would suppose, would come the *idea* of love, suggested
by her name; but Carroll by a clever stroke turns her into
a termagant, shifting the emphasis from the unitive passion
of the heart to the divisive one of anger—Cunning Old
Fury indeed. In the same way, as Mr. Empson points out,
the Tiger-lily (which Carroll originally named the
Passion Flower until it was pointed out to him that this
might be construed as irreverence, since it is Christ's
Passion to which the name refers) is moved to one passion
only, that of fury.

In the Alices the game continues, unaffected by love,
as is right and proper, the players being in this way protected from absorption in the game or absorption in one
another. Love, however, begins to creep into the Snark,
and by the time we reach *Sylvie and Bruno* it is everywhere.
The adult half of these two books is a love-story. The love
of Sylvie and Bruno, the fairy children, for one another
is a constant theme, and there is a similar bond between
them and their father, who asks Sylvie to choose between
a locket which says 'All will love Sylvie', and 'Sylvie will
love all'. Uggug, the villain, is denounced as 'loveless,
loveless!' There is a set of verses, sung by the children,
with the chorus:—

> 'For I think it is Love,
> For I feel it is Love,
> For I'm sure it is nothing but Love!'

There is an epitaph saying 'Greater love hath no man . . .'
and *Sylvie and Bruno Concluded* ends with an angel's voice
whispering (in capitals) 'IT IS LOVE.'

It is at this extreme point of insipidity and sentimen-
tality that the Sylvie and Bruno books become interesting,
not for themselves (even Carroll's devoted and reverent
nephew-biographer had doubts about the acceptability of
his uncle's mixture in these two works) but for the reason
that makes them such utter failures as Nonsense: the close
identification in them between author and subject-

matter. Carroll apparently maintained that the 'I' of the story was 'not consciously meant' to be himself (Colling-wood, *The Life and Letters of Lewis Carroll*, p. 319); but the writer of the letter from which those words are taken, a friend of Carroll's, says she finds him all the way through; and she was presumably a good judge in the matter. There can, I think, be no doubt about this, and the behaviour of the individual concerned is characteristic. He steers very clear of the adult love-interest, but develops a great love for the little fairy girl, Sylvie. He melts into sentiment, utters edifying speeches, is pious, possesses a would-be sense of humour whose manifestations are uncomfortably heavy. The most interesting point about him comes early in the first book. There his doctor friend addresses a letter to him in which the phrase occurs, 'I make no doubt he is right in saying the heart is affected: all your symptoms point that way.' This is further emphasized by the fact that the individual concerned is introduced to us reading, to beguile a railway journey, a medical work entitled *Diseases of the Heart*. One could hardly diagnose Carroll's case more clearly.

It is in a way strange that one should have arrived at this point when starting from the Snark, where the deviation from Nonsense seems to be more mental. The heart seems at first sight so much more Lear's province; and for that reason we had better go back now and look at Lear's Nonsense failures, the Nonsense songs, and wait till the next chapter to sort out the respective claims of head and heart, lunacy and poetry. The most interesting of the Nonsense songs, and the best known, are *The Owl and the Pussy-Cat, The Duck and the Kangaroo, The Daddy Long-Legs and the Fly, The Jumblies, Calico Pie* (from N.S.B.), and *The Dong with a Luminous Nose, The Pelican Chorus, The Courtship of the Yonghy-Bonghy-Bò, The Pobble Who Has No Toes*, the two Discobbolos songs and *The Quangle Wangle's Hat* (from L.L.).

One or two of these are 'failures', in this technical sense

of departures from model Nonsense practice, only in some very slight particular, and for our purposes here are less interesting than those which show a wider deviation. The Duck and the Kangaroo is an example—an incongruous pair united by affection:—

> All to follow my own dear true
> Love of a Kangaroo.

No emphasis is laid on the bond, however, and the ending is numerical and happy.

> And they hopped the whole world three times
>   round:
> And who so happy,—O who,
> As the Duck and the Kangaroo?

The same thing is true of the Quangle Wangle's Hat. There is a slight sense of loneliness, the Quangle Wangle complaining that he does not get much company. But this is only a momentary lapse, between the orthodox Nonsense beginning of the song:—

> For his Hat was a hundred and two feet wide,

and the orthodox ending with its list of incongruous creatures: Stork, Duck, Owl, Snail, Bumble-Bee, small Olympian bear, Attery Squash, Bisky Bat and so on. Again, the ending is a happy one.

In most of these songs, however, the genuine features of Nonsense recede, ousted by the introduction of themes which cannot be turned into true Nonsense because they are compounded with emotion. A beginning of the process can be seen in the first of the Discobbolos songs:—

> There is no more trouble ahead,
> Sorrow or any such thing—
>   For Mr. and Mrs. Discobbolos!

for to say that there is to be no more sorrow with such confidence is in some obscure way to disquiet the heart which knows that such a future is not possible in this world, even if the world be reduced to the narrow dimensions of the top of a wall. The same feeling is there at the end of the *Daddy Long-Legs and the Fly*, where the two beings seek an escape from pain by sailing over the sea,

> And reached the great Gromboolian plain;
> And there they play for evermore
> At battlecock and shuttle door.

They try to escape into a game, but before, in the earlier verses of what is to my mind the loveliest of the Nonsense songs, another note has been introduced which, as in the Discobbolos lines, suddenly catches the heart with a sense of reality. It is a theme which is so common throughout Lear's Nonsense that it must have a personal significance for its author. It forms a link between this Nonsense song and Lear's autobiographical verses. In the latter he says, 'Long ago he was one of the singers, But now he is one of the dumbs.' In this song the Daddy Long-Legs says:—

> 'For years I cannot hum a bit,
>   Or sing the smallest song;
> And this the dreadful reason is,
>   My legs are grown too long!'

But the Fly is equally in trouble:—

> 'If I had six long legs like yours,
>   At once I'd go to court!
> But oh! I can't, because *my* legs
>   Are so extremely short.'

A sense of physical inadequacy must have been one of Lear's characteristics. In the Nonsense proper it is turned to good account, for distortion and disproportion of bodily features are a good line in the game. In the Autobiography it is simply stated:—

> His nose is remarkably big;
> His visage is more or less hideous,
>   His beard it resembles a wig . . .

> His body is perfectly spherical . . .

But in the *Daddy Long-Legs and the Fly* there is real distress,

> 'My six long legs, all here and there,
>   Oppress my bosom with despair,'

and the theme occurs again, with the same sense of suppressed pain, in *The Courtship of the Yonghy-Bonghy-Bò* (perhaps the *Court* to which the Floppy Fly could not go, because he was not physically presentable, a Court with its King and Queen, was of the same kind?),

> 'Though you've such a tiny body,
>   And your head so large doth grow . . .
> Though you're such a Hoddy Doddy . . .'

It is there also in the *Pobble Who Has No Toes*:—

> And when he came to observe his feet,
> Formerly garnished with toes so neat
> His face at once became forlorn
> On perceiving that all his toes were gone!

It may also be there in the story of the Dong, who

> . . . wove him a wondrous Nose,—
> A Nose as strange as a Nose could be!

perhaps also in the story of the Jumblies who had green heads and blue hands. And in the Dong and the Bò and to a lesser extent in *Calico Pie* there is a real sense of personal loss and bereavement, a loss no less painful because it is the loss of something never possessed. 'They never came back to me!' There is an endlessness about it which is very like life, and very unlike Nonsense, a long age of desolation:—

> From the Coast of Coromandel,
>   Did that Lady never go;
>   On that heap of stones she mourns
>   For the Yonghy-Bonghy-Bò.
> On that Coast of Coromandel,
> In his jug without a handle
>   Still she weeps, and daily moans;
>   On that little heap of stones
>   To her Dorking Hens she moans,
> For the Yonghy-Bonghy-Bò.

. . . While ever he seeks, but seeks in vain
To meet with his Jumbly Girl again;
Lonely and wild—all night he goes,—
The Dong with a Luminous Nose!

This resembles the later work of Carroll in that so much
of the author has got into the work that it ceases to be
Nonsense. Here too, 'the heart is affected', not merely
the heart of the writer, but that of the reader as well.
There is a note of pathos in these songs, sometimes in the
most unlikely places:—

And above the wail of the Chimp and Snipe
You may hear the squeak of his plaintive pipe
(*The Dong*)

The Pobble who has no toes
    Was placed in a friendly bark,
And they rowed him back, and carried him up
    To his Aunt Jobiska's park.
And she made him a feast at his earnest wish
Of eggs and buttercups fried with fish;—
And she said,—'It's a fact the whole world knows,
That Pobbles are happier without their toes.'
(*The Pobble*)

The water it soon came in, it did,
    The water it soon came in;
So to keep them dry, they wrapped their feet
In a pinky paper all folded neat,
    And they fastened it down with a pin.
And they passed the night in a crockery-jar,
And each of them said, 'How wise we are!'
(*The Jumblies*)

If one had known nothing about Lear, one could have
guessed him to be a lonely unhappy man. As it is, the
facts are known—the loneliness, the inability to settle in
one place, the lack of self-confidence, the warm-hearted
being ('He has many friends, laymen and clerical,' *Autobiography*) who never married. One is only too well aware
of this personality in the Nonsense songs, and the curious
and interesting thing is that one agrees to let it work upon
oneself. This is important, for it is the reverse of what

happens in Carroll's later work. Carroll can write about love till he is blue in the face, and we will concede him nothing, not a breath of our own personal emotions. Lear only mentions it occasionally, and then in Nonsense fashion:—

> 'Gaze upon the rolling deep
> (Fish is plentiful and cheap)
> As the sea, my love is deep!'
> Said the Yonghy-Bonghy-Bò.

but we will give him our confidence and agree to let him work on our emotions whereas to Carroll dripping loving verbiage from his pen we will allow not one square inch of the heart. What can account for the difference?

We may come at it, perhaps, by going one stage further back and so arriving at the first and most famous of the Lear Nonsense Songs, *The Owl and the Pussy-Cat*. This is a love story—'O lovely Pussy! O Pussy, my love', with a happy ending and perhaps a significant one; for it ends with a marriage. Alongside it we may set that other curiously similar pair of Carroll's invention, the Owl and the Panther from Wonderland. This is the second verse of ' 'Tis the voice of the lobster' (a parody, as we may do well to remember, though we cannot attend to that point now). The verse is not as well remembered as its predecessor, and I give it below:—

> I passed by his garden, and marked, with one eye,
> How the Owl and the Panther were sharing a pie:
> The Panther took pie-crust, and gravy, and meat,
> While the Owl had the dish as its share of the treat.
> When the pie was all finished, the Owl, as a boon,
> Was kindly permitted to pocket the spoon:
> While the Panther received knife and fork with a growl,
> And concluded the banquet by——

At that point, where there is only one possible, if bloodthirsty, ending to the verse, Alice is interrupted, and the final fatal words are never spoken.

I do not want to make these parallel creations of the

imagination into allegories of their respective creators, nor to embark on an interpretation of them. It is interesting, none the less, that each should have paired off his owl with a feline in this way, the one with a pussy-cat, the other with a panther, and still more interesting that Lear should have envisaged the marriage of the two, while Carroll so greatly feared the destruction of the one by the other that he would not even set it down in black and white and look at it. Any idea of protecting the tender susceptibilities of his child readers from so unpleasant an ending is bunkum. We have already seen that in favourable circumstances children swallow far worse happenings without a qualm. It seems more likely that wherever Carroll in his work shies away from something it is not his readers he is protecting but himself.

There is a slight temptation to translate Owl and Pussy-Cat/Panther into psychological terms: would they not make an excellent Animus and Anima, for instance? But we had better stick to our own game; and in the terms of a game, we might perhaps take this pair of figures as the two sides of the game in Nonsense, the side of the mind which is orderly and can be played with, and the disorderly side which cannot. I myself used as a figure the phrase that one cannot play tig with a jaguar; but a panther would do just as well. It is fierce, overwhelming and uncontrollable; and that is exactly as it should be. This side of life should be all those things, and the great carnivores are good symbols for these forces which we do not well understand, cannot control and into whose grasp we are given from time to time. The devil has been compared to a roaring lion (1 Peter v) but God has been no less so: 'Thou huntest me as a fierce lion' (Job x. 16). It is no good being hunted by a pussy-cat. One would merely come back to the Nursery Rhyme position, 'The cat's in the cupboard and can't see me,' if one could shut it up there oneself, just as the Old Man on some rocks shut up his wife for the rest of her days.

Possibly, then, one may guess that Carroll had a panther in his make-up and was mortally afraid that it would eat the owl, that traditional bird of wisdom and knowledge— even perhaps of mathematics; so Merlyn's owl in the *Sword in the Stone* is called Archimedes. Lear merely has a pussy-cat; and with this his owl achieves a marriage of some sort. We need not concern ourselves with the somewhat Freudian conclusions that might be drawn from such a hypothesis. What matters to us is the effect this may have on the game, what the nature of the union or disunion is in each case, and what can be deduced from it.

Chapter 13

'DODGFATHER, DODGSON & COO'

ANY MIND that is going to attempt either a union or a complete disunion between its two sides, of order and disorder, and to express that in words, is not going to continue to write pure Nonsense. The reason for this is clear, since Nonsense is a game which requires opposition between the two forces, not the reconciliation of the two nor the complete suppression of one or other.

Union between the two is rather like those mediæval treaties where a royal wedding composed the differences of war, and the game came to an end. In the mind, a reconciliation of these two forces may produce two results. The first is sanity; for the really sane individual is not the completely rational and logical being but the one who can be fully rational and fully irrational, rejoice in both states and balance them in the middle. True Nonsense, as we have seen, is sane enough, for although it sides with order against disorder, it needs the latter for its antagonist and aims at keeping it engaged, not at suppressing it. We are still concerned for the present, however, with Nonsense failures, and it is here that the difference between Lear and Carroll becomes really sharp.

Sanity is one of Lear's outstanding characteristics, no matter whether in his Nonsense (successful or otherwise), in what one knows of his private life, in his letters. Nobody to my knowledge has ever suggested that the man who called himself Queery-Leary was queer in his head. Comments such as, 'It is easy to guess that there was something seriously wrong in his sex life' [1] are dropped now and again, but they do not carry any suggestion of derange-

[1] George Orwell, *Shooting an Elephant*, Essay on *Nonsense Poetry*, p. 181.

ment. Any such suggestion would be impossible to maintain in face of his work, above all, perhaps, of his letters,
where he laughs at himself, his feelings, his art—'my
Eggzibission', at circumstances—'Yours retched me here
(spelling adapted to circumstances)'; at pomp and cir-
cumstance—'A. Tennyson has written an im', or this
phrase about the rich: 'Patent, shiny, lacquer, pimmy-
puny tic tic tic tic'; at the Bible, where his attitude is very
different from Carroll's, as we shall see—'the great lieu-
tenant whou thou hast made to take his pastime therein';
and who at the back of all this is obviously so good a
friend—'Project all your uncomfortablenesses into my ear
and buzzim'—'Don't pollygize about your not writing: I
gnoo how bizzy u were'; and who now and again makes
such a remark as 'If you have a wife or are in love with
a woman' (both phases of the same state of self-division,
the only real and proper state of life in this world) . . .' [1]
One remembers Carroll's comment on the same subject,
also in a letter:—

> So you have been for twelve years a married man, while
> I am still a lonely old bachelor! And mean to keep so, for
> the matter of that. College life is by no means unmixed
> misery, though married life has no doubt many charms to
> which I am a stranger.
>
> (Letter to Mr. Atkinson, no date given;
>   quoted by Collingwood, *op. cit.*, p. 231.)

If sanity is the first result of this union between order
and disorder in the mind, there is a second possible one.
This, however, would depend on the union finding its
way into words, and on there being something more than
a pussy-cat to take the role of the other partner: for this
second result is poetry, which can hold both sides of a
human being in a brief but perfect equilibrium. Lear fulfils
the first condition but not the second, and so never quite
reaches poetry. This applies only to the Nonsense songs, of

[1] Letter to Chichester Fortescue, May 1st, 1859.

course, the part of his work which is not just pure Nonsense. The classic product, the limericks and stories, are
play and nothing more, which rules poetry out. But if he
never quite reaches poetry in the Songs, how near to it he
comes! It is partly that he echoes other poets, not in the
sense of plagiarism but because he, as a shadow, puts us
in mind over and over again of the reality. There is a hint
of Spenser's *Epithalamion* phrase, 'That al the woods shal
answer, and theyr eccho ring' in the *Dong*:—

> And the rocks are smooth and grey,
> And all the woods and the valleys rang
> With the Chorus they daily and nightly sang.

It is typical that Lear's poem is not even a prothalamion.
The ending of the *Owl and the Pussy-Cat*,

> And hand in hand, on the edge of the sand,
> They danced by the light of the moon,

might be first cousin to

> Come unto these yellow sands,
> And then take hands . . .
> Foot it featly here and there.

or that other moonlit dance in *Comus*,

> The Sounds, and Seas with all their finny drove
> Now to the Moon in wavering Morrice move,
> And on the tawny Sands and Shelves
> Trip the pert fairies . . .

The minute setting and detail of *The Daddy Long-Legs
and the Fly* might be Drayton, and the ending of it is
Verlaine:—

> And there they found a little boat
> Whose sails were pink and grey

> D'une lune rose et grise

In *The Jumblies* one stumbles upon Yeats, 'That dolphin-
torn, that gong-tormented sea':—

And all night long they sailed away . . .
To the echoing sound of a coppery gong . . .

Behind the Yonghy-Bonghy-Bò's 'sunset isles of Boshen'
lie Avalon and the Islands of the Blest, just as behind the
Bò's voyage through the sea on a turtle lurks the old image
of the poet on his dolphin. Lear in one of his letters
suggests hiring himself a porpoise on which to cross
the Channel. Carroll's comment on a porpoise is very
different:—

> 'There's a porpoise close behind us, and he's
> treading on my tail.'

> 'If I'd been the whiting,' said Alice, whose thoughts
> were still running on the song, 'I'd have said to the
> porpoise "Keep back, please! We don't want *you* with us!" '
> (*The Lobster-Quadrille*, A.A.W.)

Behind the idea of the turtle shell, too, on which the Bò
voyaged, comes the idea of the first instrument of poetry—
'When Jubal struck the chorded shell'. Mythology seems
to lie close behind these Songs of Lear; but there are also
passages which can stand as near-poetry in their own
right:—

> And all night long they sailed away;
>   And when the sun went down,
> They whistled and warbled a moony song
> To the echoing sound of a coppery gong,
>   In the shade of the mountains brown.
> (*The Jumblies*)

> When awful darkness and silence reign
> Over the great Gromboolian plain
>   Through the long, long wintry nights;—
> When the angry breakers roar
> As they beat on the rocky shore;—
>   When Storm-clouds brood on the towering heights
> Of the Hills of the Chankly Bore.

> They danced in circlets all night long
> To the plaintive pipe of the lively Dong,
>   In moonlight, shine or shade.
> (*The Dong With a Luminous Nose*)

By day we fish, and at eve we stand
On long bare islands of yellow sand.
And when the sun sinks slowly down
And the great rock walls grow dark and brown,
Where the purple river rolls fast and dim
And the Ivory Ibis starlike skim,
Wing to wing we dance around

. . . .

And echoing back from the rocks you heard
Multitude-echoes from Bird and Bird.

(*The Pelican Chorus*)

Does he beat his wife with a gold-topped pipe,
When she let the gooseberries grow too ripe?

(*The Akond of Swat*)

And with that we leave Lear, who, when he takes us
out of the world of Nonsense as he does in the Songs,
takes us to the happy borders of poetry. The reader's
confidence in the world to which he is admitted in the
Nonsense proper, or in that of the Nonsense songs, is
never for one moment shaken. I daresay Carroll would
have liked to be thought of as a poet too. Unlike Lear, he
makes a number of deliberate poetic attempts; the following are typical:—

He sat beside the busy street,
    There, where he last had seen her face;
And thronging memories, bitter-sweet,
    Seemed yet to haunt the ancient place:
Her footfall ever floated near:
Her voice was ever in his ear.

(*Three Sunsets*)

Then once again the solemn whisper came:
'So in the darkest path of man's despair,
Where War and Terror shake the troubled earth,
Lies woman's mission; with unblenching brow
To pass through scenes of horror and affright.'

(*The Path of Roses*)

A sweet pale child—
Wearily looking to the purple West—

M

Waiting the great For-ever
That suddenly shall sever
The cruel chains that hold her from her rest—
By earth-joys unbeguiled.

(Stolen Waters)

It is plain that wherever Carroll leads us, it is not into poetry, and we have now to collect up our various clues about the man and try to put them together.

They seem at first sight conflicting, at least if they are taken at their extremes, and we find Virginia Woolf, for instance, saying,

> None of the transitions in Alice in Wonderland is quite so queer. For we wake to find—is it the Rev. C. L. Dodgson? Is it Lewis Carroll? Or is it both combined? This conglomerate object intends to produce an extra-Bowdlerised edition of Shakespeare for the use of British maidens; implores them to think of death when they go to the play; and always, always to realize that 'the true object of life is the development of *character* . . .'. Is there, even in 1293 pages, any such thing as 'completeness'?
>
> (Essay on *Lewis Carroll* in *The Moment*, p. 71)

'Dual nature', 'discrepancy' are words that crop up frequently in connection with Carroll-Dodgson; but it seems very unsatisfactory to leave one individual in two such watertight compartments. One answer might be schizophrenia, but for lay-people that is merely to give another name to a not very clearly understood acquiescence in one person being two. It is not going to be the answer here in any case, partly because it is a psychological term and therefore outside our terms of reference, partly because it does not solve our problem. Admittedly I said in Chapter 10 that the Snark is disturbing because it feels a little mad (and oddly enough the illustrators who have dealt with this work, Harry Furniss and, in our own time, Mervyn Peake, do nothing to reassure us on this point). But the trouble is not that that work shows a split; it is that it does not. So with Carroll himself—there are suggestions already that Dodgson and Carroll are very much one and the same being. We have seen that the marriage of Owl and Pussy-Cat produced sanity. Here we have Owl and Panther, unmarried, indeed on the contrary the one fearing destruction by the other, and we had better go back to the Snark and find out what the nature of the disunion is.

The last chapter dealt with the numerous ways in which the Snark breaks the rules of the Nonsense game. It is noticeable that the breach in each case takes the same form: that of permitting the entrance, into what is ostensibly still a game, of something that has no place in a game and should be kept out. It is for this very purpose that games surround themselves with their elaborate limitations and rules. Dreams, delirium, madness, the infinity of nothingness, emotions are all allowed into the Snark. These are unsuited to a game, but that is not to deny their reality as notions or factors in existence; and that is just the trouble. For, with them, real life breaks into the game where it has no business to be. As if this were not enough of a breach in the playground fence, two other aspects of real life which we have not dealt with yet are allowed in also. The first is the complex organization of the contemporary civilized world. The Stock Exchange is admitted, with the Broker and the railway share; the business of banking, with the Banker, the changing of loose silver into notes, the offer of a cheque 'Drawn to bearer for seven pounds ten'; insurance, when the Beaver is offered two policies, one against fire and one against damage from hail; organized charity, meetings, collections and subscribers; the whole rigmarole of legal proceedings in Fit the Sixth, a very different matter from the inconsequent trial in Wonderland; and two references to social canons—introductions and invitations to dinner-parties.

This is what Mr. E. M. Forster has called in a wonderful phrase the life of telegrams and anger; and along with the material complications of civilization and the social emotions come social ethics in the Snark. The names of one after another human quality and virtue are introduced, and it is interesting to see what happens to them, for it is characteristic of this work and important for the understanding of Carroll as a whole. For, like the Banker and the Judge and the charity meeting, they are introduced only to be mocked at.

'His form is ungainly—his intellect small—'
(So the Bellman would often remark)—
'But his courage is perfect! And that, after all,
Is the thing that one needs with a Snark!'
(Fit the First)

The Bellman himself they all praised to the skies—
Such a carriage, such ease and such grace!
Such solemnity, too! One could see he was wise,
The moment one looked in his face!

.   .   .   .

This was charming, no doubt: but they shortly found out
That the Captain they trusted so well
Had only one notion for crossing the ocean,
And that was to tingle his bell.
(Fit the Second)

'For England expects—I forbear to proceed:
'Tis a maxim tremendous, but trite.'
(Fit the Fourth)

This is strange when one comes to think about it. Obviously there is no need to adopt a priggish attitude and claim that courage and wisdom and so on are sacred and inviolable; they are not, but neither they nor mockery of them can be regarded as suitable material for a game. If they come in they should be treated exactly like any other quality, stated but unemphasized and unridiculed, on a level with having a huge hat or no toes. Here is courage in Lear:—

There was a Young Lady of Hull,
Who was chased by a virulent Bull;

But she seized on a spade, and called out—
   'Who's afraid!'
Which distracted that virulent Bull.

(B.N.)

It is stated but not scouted, and takes its place as one of the normal parts of the Nonsense universe, no more and no less valuable than any other.

We come now to a point that has been waiting for us for some time—Carroll's use of parody. Its importance for the moment is that it suggests that the root of this uncertainty in the Snark, this introduction and ridiculing of real life, is present from the very beginning of Carroll's work, since there are parodies in the Alices. The poems which Carroll selected for parody in *Wonderland* and *Looking-Glass* are moral and high-toned. His productions stand on their own feet in those works, of course, for readers will not necessarily know that Old Father William comes from Southey, or the White Knight's Aged, Aged Man from Wordsworth's *Resolution and Independence*, or *'Tis the voice of the Lobster* from Isaac Watts. What we receive from Carroll in these cases is Nonsense of the very best kind:—

> Yet you balanced an eel on the end of your nose—
> What made you so awfully clever?

> But I was thinking of a plan
>   To dye one's whiskers green,
> And always use so large a fan
>   That they could not be seen.

Yet it is worth casting an eye at the originals.

> You are old, Father William, the young man cried;
>   And life must be hastening away;
> You are cheerful and love to converse upon death!
>   Now tell me the reason I pray.

> I am cheerful, young man, Father William replied,
>   Let the cause thy attention engage:
> In the days of my youth I remember'd my God!
>   And He hath not forgotten my age.

That is Southey's *The Old Man's Comforts*. The Wordsworth poem is a long one, and Carroll has made less exact
a parody of it, though certain lines such as 'How is it
that you live, and what is it you do?' occur in each. The
following is a sample of the Wordsworth:—

> He told, that to these waters he had come
> To gather Leeches, being old and poor:
> Employment hazardous and wearisome!
> And he had many hardships to endure;
> From pond to pond he roamed, from moor to moor;
> Housing, with God's good help, by choice or chance;
> And in this way he gained an honest maintenance.

It is curious that Carroll should have chosen these two,
with their mention of God, for travesty. Mr. Empson
comments on this:—

> Dodgson was fond of saying that one parodied the best
> poems, or anyway that parody showed no lack of admira-
> tion, but a certain bitterness is inherent in parody; if the
> meaning is not 'This poem is absurd' it must be 'In my
> present mood of emotional sterility the poem will not work,
> or I am afraid to let it work, on *me*.'
>
> (*Some Versions of the Pastoral*, p. 263)

There is something that might be added to this, for
parody besides being a mockery of the original is at the
same time a recognition of it. Even though in the Alices
the reality or original is kept right out of the picture, it
is there in Carroll's mind. Lear writes no parody; he does
not recognize this dangerous thing called real life or does
not fear it. Carroll's mockery looks as if it were some kind
of defence, and the process is not confined to the parodies
in the works. Consider, for instance, the implicit mockery
of beauty in 'Beautiful Soup', or of majesty in Carroll's
Kings and Queens, the former, whether of Hearts or of
White or Red Chesspieces, ineffectual and vacillating, the
latter viragoes, vinegary governesses or stupid old sheep.
Lear only has one mention of king and queen, but they are
perfectly seemly and dignified, if in Nonsense terms:—

> ... the King and Queen
> (One in red, and one in green)
> Would say aloud, 'You are not fit,
> You Fly, to come to court a bit!'
> (*The Daddy Long-Legs and the Fly*)

In the Alices we are not asked to look at whatever it is that Carroll is defending himself from; in the Snark the reality and the defence are both there, in an uneasy mixture; and by the time we get to *Sylvie and Bruno*, the defence has vanished altogether, and life is both real and earnest.

A number of critics have made Carroll out to be, as far as the Alices at least were concerned, a pioneer of the liberation of children from the moral works which were considered suitable juvenile reading before his time. If this is so, they still have to explain the extraordinary metamorphosis of that liberator into the writer of the Preface to *Sylvie and Bruno* which has already figured in the extract from Virginia Woolf, and in which appear the ominous words:—

> It is written, not for money, and not for fame, but in the hope of supplying, for the children whom I love, some thoughts that may suit those hours of innocent merriment which are the very life of Childhood: and also, in the hope of suggesting, to them and to others, some thoughts that may prove, I would fain hope, not wholly out of harmony with the graver cadences of life.

The solemnity of the whole of this preface is most interesting. Carroll talks about a project for a children's Bible and an additionally expurgated Shakespeare; from this we pass to thoughts of death, immorality at the theatre, blood sports and the heinousness of their pursuit by women, whom Carroll does not name but calls 'those *"tender and delicate"* beings, whose very name serves as a symbol of Love'; and we end with thoughts of the Love of God. How can this be reconciled with the parodies we have just been looking at, which indirectly mock at God, of Whose susceptibilities the Rev. C. L. Dodgson was so careful that he would allow no connection whatever between humour and religion to be made in his presence?

We need not look for a psychological explanation, but can come at it by remembering the importance of the principles of selection and exclusion in a game. In the Alices the game goes forward without our being troubled necessarily even with the memory of the pious and moral originals lying behind so many of the verses. The exclusion is properly maintained; but the root is there already of that later development which was to produce the dreadful hodge-podge of *Sylvie and Bruno*. It is there by the very fact that Carroll chose to incorporate parody in his Nonsense and that he chose such originals to work on. There was no compulsion on him. Nonsense can reach its goal without parody, and perhaps reach it better. Carroll's first stage, in the Alices, is, 'I will take this nobility and high-mindedness and convert it into suitable material for a game, sugaring the hair, boiling bridges in wine and so on. We will look at the latter and suppress or overlay the former.' In the Snark, the position is, 'I will treat nobility and high-mindedness as if they were suitable material for a game, and will play with that and the rest of my material together, forks and hope, courage and hyenas side by side.' Already here too much is getting in. We do not want courage and so on in a game, nor the Stock Exchange, nor dreams. They are out of place and pervert the game in the direction of reality, whether mocked at or not, since the mockery serves only to emphasize their presence. The third attitude, with *Sylvie and Bruno*, is, 'Here is real life, grave thoughts, beauty, love, God, railway journeys, epidemics, alcoholism, the Oxford Movement, and they are all suitable matter for Nonsense, but the game must now be sober and reverent.' There can be only one result; the game dies, and instead the reader is left with a dreary, odious and pretentious mixture of false sentiment, preaching and whimsy.

The point at the moment is not the reader, however; it is Carroll himself. An explanation of the disquiet we feel at the Snark and the disgust at *Sylvie and Bruno* is coming to light. We said, when the idea of a game was first mooted, that compulsion is foreign to the nature of play. Someone, however, might perhaps compel themselves to play, extending the game more and more widely till it tried to take in the whole of life. So far we have been looking at the intrusions which have broken into the Nonsense game with the Snark and Sylvie. We could perfectly well think of it the other way round, however, as an attempt on the part of the player to remove the landmarks of the game further and further out, not because this improves the game (in fact it destroys it) but because the said player cannot live without the sense of safety which a game gives, cannot cope with reality on any other terms than those of a game and so must squeeze everything into this charmed circle where the player is in control. It is, of course, a vicious circle, for the attempt to increase security in this way merely destroys the exclusiveness by which a game achieves its safety. We are left with the spectacle of a mind camping for ever and ever inside its would-be game, never daring to venture out of it, and devoid of all the mobility and free movement necessary for play.

Mobility and free movement of the mind are not only necessary for play, however, but for sanity as well. A mind must be able to move from one of its systems to another. It must at times act as agent in logic and order, and at other times as patient in disorder, emotion and dream. We can see fairly clearly that anyone sitting down for good and all in a dream world has gone mad; the symptoms in such a case are fairly obvious. It is not quite so obvious, perhaps (because we set greater store by rationality than irrationality), that anyone refusing to leave the field of logic and order is equally unbalanced, and equally far from reality which demands unconditionally a readiness to be played with as well as to play. Owl and Panther have to come to terms somehow; but Carroll was afraid of the Panther even by the time he wrote his first Nonsense book, and the progressive deterioration of his relations with it can be seen in the later works. Part of the unpleasantness of the two *Sylvie and Bruno* works is the spectacle of a grown man playing or play-acting at emotion, at ethics, at religion, refusing to see that that is what he is doing.

> *I* felt very happy too, but of course I didn't cry: 'big things' never do, you know— . . . Only I think it must have been raining a little just then, for I found a drop or two on my cheeks.
>
> > (*Bruno's Revenge*, s.b.)

> Fading, with the Night, the memory of a dead love, and the withered leaves of a blighted hope, and the sickly repinings and moody regrets that numb the best energies of the soul: and rising, broadening, rolling upwards like a living flood, the manly resolve, and the dauntless will, and the heavenward gaze of faith.
>
> > (*Looking Eastward*, s.b.)

> 'Muriel—my love——' he paused, and his lips quivered: but after a minute he went on more steadily. 'Muriel—my darling—they—*want* me—down in the harbour.'
> '*Must* you go?' she pleaded . . . looking up into his face with her great eyes brimming over with tears. 'Must *you* go, Arthur? It may mean—death!'
> He met her gaze without flinching. 'It *does* mean death, he said in a husky whisper: 'but—darling—I am *called*.'
>
> > (*To the Rescue!* s.b.c.)

It is not just the style that is at fault here; it is the insincerity of the tone, leading the reader to surmise that the man behind these passages was shut off from the reality which he chooses to write about. There is an interesting example of this very thing in the two sets of verses which Carroll wrote about the baby daughter of a friend of his. (Carroll detested babies.) For an official collection of

tributes to the newcomer entitled *The Garland of Rachel*,
he produced seven typical verses, beginning,

> What hand may wreathe thy natal crown,
>   O tiny tender Spirit-blossom,
> That out of Heaven hast fluttered down
>   Into this Earth's cold bosom?

But the other poem began very differently:—

> Oh pudgy podgy pup!
> Why *did* they wake you up?
> Those crude nocturnal yells
> Are *not* like silver bells.

That has the merit of being honest, but there is little of
this conformity between man and work. For behind the
emotional passages, the pious passages, what Mr. Empson
has called the 'hysterical passages on vivisection', there
lurks this, in Collingwood's words:—

> In one respect Lewis Carroll resembled the stoic philoso-
> phers, for no outward circumstance could upset the
> tranquillity of his mind. He lived, in fact, the life which
> Marcus Aurelius commends so highly, the life of calm
> contentment . . . But in him there was one exception to
> this rule. During an argument he was often excited. The
> war of words, the keen and subtle conflict between trained
> minds—in this his soul took delight, in this he sought and
> found the joy of battle and of victory. Yet he would not
> allow his serenity to be ruffled by any foe whom he con-
> sidered unworthy of his steel; he refused to argue with
> people whom he knew to be hopelessly illogical.
>
> (Op. cit., pp. 271–2)

It is a most revealing passage, the more so because the
biographer was unconscious of any revelation. It is interesting that the one thing by which Carroll allowed
himself to be excited was dialectic, which is all part of a
game. Presumably he felt himself so safe here and so much
on his own ground that the panther was allowed out occasionally for a little run.

His delight in argument has one significant exception, however. He writes to Miss Edith Rix, on January 15th, 1886, 'I have a deep dread of argument on religious topics: it has many risks, and little chance of doing good. You and I will never *argue*, I hope, on any controverted religious question' (Collingwood, p. 251). This is another indication of how carefully Carroll kept his religion and his game apart. Taken in isolation, refusal to argue on religious matters might not seem so unreasonable a line to take. But how about the following?—

> . . . while the laughter of *joy* is in full harmony with our deeper life, the laughter of amusement should be kept apart from it. The danger is too great of thus learning to look at solemn things in a spirit of *mockery*, and to seek in them opportunities for exercising *wit*. That is the spirit which has spoiled, for me, the beauty of some of the Bible.
> (Letter to Miss Dora Abdy, no date given,
> Collingwood, p. 331)

> The favour I ask is, that you will not tell me any more stories, such as you did on Friday, of remarks which children are said to have made on very sacred subjects . . . The hearing of that anecdote gave me so much pain, and spoiled so much the pleasure of my tiny dinner-party, that I feel sure you will kindly spare me such in future. . . . there is no surer way of making one's beliefs *unreal* than by learning to associate them with ludicrous ideas.
> (Letter to an unnamed friend, 1897;
> Collingwood, pp. 237–8)

> A letter of protest was sent, of all people, by Lewis Carroll to my father deprecating the introduction of any element of amusement into a sermon.
> (Letter quoted by Langford Reed,
> *The Life of Lewis Carroll*, Ch. X, p. 105)

Langford Reed maintains that on religious matters there was no difference of opinion whatever between Lewis

Carroll and the Rev. C. L. Dodgson. But it seems likely that there was no split between them at all, on any subject. The problem is merely this: what made Carroll so desperately anxious to keep Lewis Carroll and Dodgson, Nonsense and Religion, separate? The passages quoted above show one thing clearly. The attitude may seem to us ridiculous, but there is no question about the reality of the pain and fear at the back of the man's mind, a terror of any rapprochement between these two sides of life. There is some deep-seated insecurity; why otherwise should he insist on keeping laughter and dialectic away from their Author, as if He had to be protected from His Own inventions? The answer seems to be that it is not God Who is being protected but Carroll. There is only one way in which he can protect himself—and that is a disturbing one.

The attempt to deal with the whole of life in terms of a game has other consequences than the more obvious ones, such as, for instance, in Carroll's case, the refusal to marry and the forming of numerous rather emotional friendships with little girls whom he dropped as soon as they began to grow up, that is, as soon as they became capable of making demands on him. For even in a small game the player has to remain in control. If more and more gets into the game, he is in a difficulty, but he still has to maintain the appearance of being in command. He must always be in action, never in passivity, for that is to allow the initiative to slip to something or somebody else, to be in potentiality to the partner or opponent in the game. To be always in action, however, and to rule out all passion and potentiality, is not the part of a human being. It is, according to Saint Thomas, the part of God. 'God is pure act, and without any potentiality' (*Summa*, Pt. I, Q. 3, Art. 2). I do not want to suggest that Carroll thought he was God. He could only have done that if he had gone mad in the other direction, so to speak, in the direction of dream and disorder. It is simply that two cannot play this particular game, and if Carroll was playing it, God could not play it also in Carroll's scheme of things. Carroll abandoned the flexibility of his mind and chose to remain imprisoned inside his own game for fear of being asked to surrender himself in any way. His own Church's presentation of God was not of the kind which requires total submission of the intellect to revealed dogma. Such a thing would no doubt have horrified him. As it was, he could rub along on fairly vague notions. 'More and more it seems to me (I hope you won't be *very* much shocked at me as an ultra "Broad" Churchman) that what a person *is* is of more importance in God's sight than what propositions he affirms or denies' (letter to Miss Edith Rix, January 15th, 1886; Collingwood, p. 251).

Even so, he had two incompatible notions in his mind, and his efforts to keep them apart and the fear and pain they caused him spring from this, the distress being all the greater because, in such a case, the sufferer cannot account for the extent and intensity of the pain involved. If Carroll is to play with the whole of his life, always to be in control of it as a player must be, and as none other can, then he must be his own God. His passion to separate God and his game is not for the sake of the Deity but in order to keep God off Carroll's preserves. It is most interesting that James Joyce in *Finnegans Wake* should have produced the extraordinary identification which heads this chapter, the phrase 'Dodgfather, Dodgson & Coo', which unites the notions of the Holy Trinity, Carroll, dodging, and a limited liability company.

We are safe with Lear because he is himself safe. Pussy-Cat or not, the marriage was made, and the sanity which results from it turns upon those three things, laughter, poetry and religion, inwardly experienced and whole-hearted, which reappear here in tantalizing combination when we cannot hope to work out their inter-relationship. We can only suppose that they have some affinity, each working out its own form of union and balance in the mind. It is a strange conclusion to come to, but as far as one can see, Carroll never came near the reality of any of them. This man who was in Holy Orders in the Anglican Church and who is presented to us by his contemporaries as deeply religious has only to open his mouth to convince us of the insecurity of his beliefs. This man who wrote much would-be poetry convinces us, by that, that he does not begin to understand poetry's nature. And strangest of all, it looks as if the inventor of Alice had no sense of humour. He was a brilliant player of a particular game, but that is not at all the same thing. In each of these three spheres he played his own game which he meant to control; and that is not religion, nor is it laughter (where humour must be directed against oneself as well as against others), nor is it poetry.

Equally, however, it is not sanity. Those were Lear's answers, separately and in conjunction. Carroll's is the remark he lends to Alice, 'I don't want to be anybody's prisoner,' and by a dreadful irony he thereby imprisons himself for ever inside his own game where he can play at being God, and the tighter the imprisonment becomes, the more the reader senses it and wants to say 'Let me out.' Some minds find it even in the Alices. Children sometimes find them frightening, and Chesterton speaks of Wonderland as 'a country populated by insane mathematicians.' Empson says that both books have a 'kinship with insanity' (*Some Versions of the Pastoral*, p. 293). Collingwood (p. 407) reports a rumour current during Carroll's lifetime that he had gone mad. One of his ex-child-friends is reported as saying of him, 'He had the brain of a clever and abnormal man with the heart of a normal child.'[1] The breath of insanity clings about him as it has never done, and could not do, about Lear. For after all, the universe is not a chess-board, the player is not God, and no human being is allowed to play for ever

[1] Langford Reed, *op. cit.*, Ch. IX, p. 95.

and with everything. That is reserved for the Wisdom that played before the face of God at the beginning of the Creation, 'ludens coram eo omni tempore: ludens in orbe terrarum', and whose playthings we may be content to be, as Dodgfather, Dodgson & Coo was not.

Chapter 14

WILL YOU, WON'T YOU?

B Y N O W we seem almost to have settled down into a closed circle of our own. We have finished playing our own game with the materials with which Nonsense provided us. We have examined its rules, worked out our own over thirteen chapters, seen where the game failed, and seen too, satisfying the mind's love of consistency, that here as in other cases, 'it is manifest that what is made is like to the maker, forasmuch as every agent makes its like' (*Summa*, Pt. I, Q. 110, Art. 2). It might be supposed that now there is no more to do but to blow the whistle and pronounce the game over: but that is the last thing that is going to happen. It would be in a way better if it did, since this is the concluding chapter, and one might suppose that a tidy finish would become it. There are, however, other ways of ending; and here we shall not lock the last link home in that safe circle of our own game, for this is the moment at which to come out of the circle and to meet whatever there may be outside, held at bay so far by the circle within which we have been moving—one of the first principles of magic. Or say that we have built a house of cards and will now finish the game by knocking it down; it will not make a scholarly last chapter, but it is a good way to end all the same, for it forbids an ending.

So far we have, like Lear and Carroll and Nonsense in general, been logical and exclusive, as if all this world were rational, and we with it. That is the right way to play this kind of game. Play seemed so safe when we started, and Nonsense too, since we chose to think of it in that way, even if it was a game with words, strangest, most brilliant and most dangerous of all man's inventions, of so high and mysterious a nature, as well as being so normal and commonplace, that they have found their way into the naming of the Trinity. Perhaps this is partly why any examination of words and of ways of using them should bring one to this point where the world ceases to be purely rational and becomes something else, something more. And if the looking into words be itself a game, and if what is being looked at is a game with words, we shall be the more surely caught. For words and play together fringe out into liturgy and magic, and that is country of a different kind.

There are suggestions of this breaking out of the circle already inside our own terms of reference. Chesterton, who had far more ideas than he ever worked out, gives a hint of it in his *Defence of Nonsense* when he says, 'The well-meaning person who, by merely studying the logical side of things, has decided that 'faith is nonsense', does not know how truly he speaks; later it may come back to him in the form that nonsense is faith' (p .197). Lear's biographer, Davidson, makes independently a similar suggestion, saying of the Nonsense world, 'The entry to it demands an act of faith such as that made by Alice when she tried to go and meet the Red Queen—of starting in the opposite direction. It is an act of faith worth making, and generously rewarded' (*op. cit.*, Ch. XIII, p. 202). This is only a hint at something, however; for the latter quotation at least suggests that what is needed in Nonsense is an act of confidence on the part of the reader, a readiness to entrust himself to such devious paths. This is not the case with true Nonsense. It is much more true of poetry, where passivity is required as well as activity, which is perhaps why so many people nowadays keep poetry at arm's length, since they are unwilling to abandon themselves to it, and so they deny it its proper ground of working. What lies behind this idea that Nonsense and faith are in some way connected? Belief as such is not required in Nonsense, any more than it is in dialectic[1] or in play. A unity and inseparability of belief and disbelief, so Huizinga says (*Homo Ludens*, Ch. I, p. 40), holds good inside play. In the Nonsense we have been studying there is no need either of belief or disbelief. We do not have to believe in the Jumblies or the blackbirds in the pie. They are in the game, and that is enough.

There is, however, another half to play. We ruled this out in Chapter 4, to keep our own circle small enough, but it cannot be kept out indefinitely, and this is the point at which it comes in, not as a foreign element but as a necessary extension and completion of our own form of play, a move away from the logic and order and manipulation of pieces inside the circle, towards whatever there may be outside, where reason may end and faith begin. These are the games of make-believe, representational play, where the armchair propped up on its front is a cave, and you are the lion inside it. It makes its appearance for a moment at the beginning of the Looking-Glass:

> And here I wish I could tell you half the things Alice used to say, beginning with her favourite phrase, 'Let's pretend'.
>
> (*Looking-Glass House*)

It is that phrase that takes Alice through the mirror: 'Let's pretend the glass has got all soft, like gauze, so that we can get through.' This says that if you pretend hard enough you can shift reality, or at least bring yourself into closer connection with hitherto inaccessible regions of it.

This is where the circle of play we have made for ourselves breaks for good and all. It is an old idea that God plays with the world, expressed in that wonderful saying of Plato's, 'One must be serious with the serious, and it is God who is worthy of all blessed seriousness, but man is really made to be the play of God and that is really the

---

[1] Cf. Mortimer J. Adler, *Dialectic*, Kegan Paul, London, 1927, p. 32, 'Stated most radically, belief is as irrelevant as facts are, to the nature of dialectical discourse.'

best thing in him' (*Laws*). The idea can go deeper than this, however, to the notion that in play there is some connection between the world and the power that rules it. Siva sits at dice with his consort, and that is an image of the world and its working, and behind many games lies magic of just this sort, divination—that expressive word. It lies behind the very games we have been treating as examples of logic and order, dice and dominoes with their numerical play, and behind board games such as chess. Of the game of dominoes it is said that 'from the cosmical associations of the pieces, and their use in divination, which continues in China to the present day, it may be regarded as having been originally used for that purpose'. Dice throws are said to represent the Four Quarters and the intermediary divisions of the world, 'implements of magic . . . corresponding with playing cards'. So cards are involved too, the four suits being originally the emblems of the Four Directions, not to mention the Tarot pack, the 'wicked pack of cards' of *The Waste Land*, which one writer at least has linked with Alice and with the phrase, 'You're nothing but a pack of cards.' In chess, too, the same tendency lurks, the board representing the world.[1]

We thought we were on safe ground with these logical games, so numbered and orderly; but Siva dices with the world, and if, in terms of mythology, the gods play games with the universe, then any play on our part is a shadowing of theirs, a game of representation and make-believe as well as the sober logical manipulation of the game proper. So any game is at one and the same time an exercise of skill and manipulative ability, a way of finding out how God deals with the universe, and a dangerous make-believe with holy things.

[1] Stewart Culin, *Chess and Playing Cards*. Report of the U.S. National Museum for the year ending June 30th, 1896, pp. 679–942. The Tarot-Alice connection is made in Muriel Bruce Hasbrouck's *Pursuit of Destiny*: with Thirty-Six Tarot Cards, E. P. Dutton & Co. Inc., New York, 1941.

At this point all the safety of the game has disappeared and we are in the world of religion, magic, alchemy, astrology, poetry and those strange riddles, oracular or monstrous, proposed to human beings as a matter of life and death (Huizinga, *Homo Ludens*, Ch. VI). Any game, no matter how logical, sets one by the mere fact of playing it in the position of make-believe and divination. Logic cannot deal with such a situation. It has nothing to say outside the little closed circle of its own activity, and could not by itself grasp such a situation—that the pursuit of a logical end could automatically lift one straight out of logic into the world of unreason and magic. Just so, any purely logical reader of this chapter will not understand this either: that to play, no matter at what, is to play at being God, and that at the end of this work on Nonsense, we seem still to have no satisfactory answer to the question: who plays the game or dreams the dream? It is as if Nonsense really were a looking-glass, and instead of knowing more about Nonsense at the end of our study we find we have merely been studying ourselves. This is interesting, however, for this is where the dream comes in, as we saw in Chapter 4 that it might do, and it gives us a clue to the answer about Lear and Carroll and their game. It is the way of working of the dream side of the mind to identify the self with other things, to say, 'I am a tree' or 'I am a railway engine,' or 'I am Sir Brian, as bold as a lion,' or, very properly, 'I am Nonsense.' So dream has after all been involved here, quite as much as logic and game, which is as it should be if the mind is to work fully, playing with logic and being played with by the dream. (It would be interesting to know whether, if we had followed the alternative dream thread through Nonsense instead of opting for the game, we should have been at the end confronted with logic.) The mind is seemingly partly the player and partly its own plaything, not alternately but simultaneously, in a mutual interchange. If this is so, it may explain the difficulty of deciding whether in a game it is necessary for the mind to know it is playing, in full consciousness. We said in Chapter 4 that consent was necessary to the game, but consciousness is more doubtful; for with which of its playing halves in this game is the mind to be conscious? It is like asking the game to be conscious of itself.

How is one to understand this? Clearly the answer does not lie in any thinking we have done so far, but in the future somewhere. One comes to see more and more clearly, not only in connection with games and Nonsense but in many other ways of thought and experience, that what we need is a way of managing that other side, the unreason and disorder and make-believe and magic. For thirteen chapters now we have been logical, only to find at the end that we need an insulation from our own logic which has landed us in the world of magic without telling us what to do there. We need some way of moving from the circle of logic to the world outside the circle, from manipulation to make-believe. Reason cannot supply it, for the game we have been studying and playing has been reasonable, and any further pursuit of logic will merely take us further into this side of the game and hence into this dilemma. The answer cannot be a rational one. Some time ago, just as I was dropping asleep, when the mind slips one or two of its cogs and puts curious things together, I found myself wondering if I could do my thinking with ivy leaves. The waking mind classes such a thought as insane, but it holds a suggestion of what is needed here. We can only work in unreason by putting things together, as is the way of the mind in this dream side of its working, enlisting if possible the help of the body as well, since as we have seen, the body has closer affinities with this side of things, or as St. Thomas says, 'the imagination is moved by sense to act' (*Summa*, Pt. I, Q. 12, Art. 3). The logical type of play is a manipulation of things, and this held good in Nonsense; but this other type of play is a putting of oneself into things, not the moving of bodies (be they cards or counters or 'abstract bodies', if one may use the phrase, such as words in the head), but perhaps something to do with the body itself, and movement.

There are some phrases in a writer which catch the imagination out of all proportion to their importance. Lear produced one of these when he wrote in a letter to Chichester Fortescue, 'I am older than Babylon' (January 11th, 1857). Babylon is Babel, that place where the builders tried to construct something that would reach to heaven, and by this drew God down to see what they were about, until He scattered them by a diversification of their language, so that the tower was never finished. Strange connections of ideas wander behind that story, the idea of the power that lies behind any unity of speech (in poetry, it might be, or incantation), and of this being an approach to what is godlike, and hence dangerous presumption. It is not only Lear who talks about Babylon.

> How many miles to Babylon?
> Three score miles and ten.
> Can I get there by candlelight?
> Yes, and back again.

There is another couplet sometimes added to that Nursery Rhyme, which goes like this:—

> If your heels are nimble and light
> You can get there by candlelight.

Carroll, too, mentions the rhyme, in *Queer Street, Number Forty* (s.b.). The quoting of it by Eric Lindon awakens the following response:—

> 'We don't want to get to *Babylon*, oo know!' Bruno explained as he swung.
> 'And it isn't *candlelight*: it's *daylight*!' Sylvie added, giving the swing a push of extra vigour . . .

Carroll does not want to go to Babylon, but then his heels were not nimble and light; that, as we have already seen, was just his trouble. He will not dance to Babylon by candlelight, but insists that it is daylight. Indeed, he will not dance at all, and all his dancers are lumpish and short of wind. Tweedledum and Tweedledee curtail their dance abruptly in *Looking-Glass*, and the dancers in *The Lobster-Quadrille* are equally clumsy: 'So they began solemnly dancing round and round Alice, every now and then treading on her toes when they passed too close.' It is understandable that Alice declines a suggested repetition of the dance. As for the song, with the 'Will you, won't you' chorus, it leaves the matter open, but we have already had a flat and frightened refusal in the second verse:—

> But the snail replied, 'Too far, too far!' and gave a look askance—
> Said he thanked the whiting kindly, but he would not join the dance.

Here is Carroll himself on the subject, writing to one of his little girls:—

> As to dancing, my dear, I *never* dance, unless I am allowed to do it *in my own peculiar way* . . . The last house I tried it in, the floor broke through. But then it was a poor sort of floor—the beams were only six inches thick, hardly worth calling beams at all; stone arches are much more sensible, when any dancing, *of my peculiar kind*, is to be done. Did you ever see the Rhinoceros and the Hippopotamus, at the Zoological Gardens, trying to dance a minuet together? It is a touching sight.
>
> (Letter to Janet Gaynor, December 26th, 1886)

This is someone whose heels are anything but nimble and light, and whose creations take after their creator. But Lear's creatures dance joyously on all occasions, with no matter what for a partner. The Owl and Pussy-Cat end by dancing, the Jumblies dance to the Dong's piping, the Pelicans dance to their own chorus, and all the creatures cavort on the Quangle-Wangle's Hat. The mice in *Calico Pie* join in,

Flippity flup,
They drank it all up
And danced in the cup.

Upside down or right way up, it is all one,

So the Ducky, and the leetle
Browny-Mousy and the Beetle
Dined, and danced upon their heads
Till they toddled to their beds.
(*The Table and the Chair*, N.S.B.)

The limerick people dance too, the Old Person of Ischia who specialized in hornpipes and jigs, the waltzing man from Skye partnered by a blue-bottle; the pigs dance to a silver-gilt flute, the Old Man of Whitehaven dances with a raven, the Old Man of the Border with his cat. Dance gives the subject for two of Lear's most delightful limericks and illustrations:—

There was an old person of Slough,
Who danced at the end of a bough;
But they said, 'If you sneeze, You might damage
   the trees,
You imprudent old person of Slough.'

There was an old person of Filey,
Of whom his acquaintance spoke highly;
He danced perfectly well, to the sound of a bell,
And delighted the people of Filey.

Nursery Rhyme, too, is full of the same spirit and movement. Some of the rhymes can themselves be danced to, such as the Good old Duke of York, or Ring-a-Roses; and references to dance are everywhere, from 'Over the hills and far away', which is about nothing else, to these smaller examples:—

Dance to your daddie,
My bonnie laddie,
Dance to your daddie, my bonnie lamb!

The cat came piping out of the barn
With a pair of bagpipes under her arm.

She would play nothing but 'Fiddledee dee!
The mouse has married the humble-bee.'
   Pipe, cat! Dance, mouse!
We'll have a wedding at our good house!

Cock a doodle doo,
My dame shall dance with you,
My master's found his fiddling-stick,
Cock a doodle doo.

I skipped over water, I danced over sea,
And all the birds of the air couldn't catch me.

Out of England he made them dance,
Out of England into France . . .

and lastly what is perhaps the loveliest example of all,
'London Bridge is broken down', with its refrain, 'Dance
over, my lady lee', and the idea behind it that where there
is no walking it may still be possible to dance.

And that is the point here. It is surprising to find ourselves emerging from Nonsense into the dance, but that is
what seems to be happening. Dance is half a game, but only
half. Games are a manipulation of things, but this is what
we were looking for just now, a kind of thinking with the
body, freedom and mobility combined with the experience
of some intuitive make-believe way of understanding
things by dancing them. Like a game, and unlike art, its
accent is on doing rather than making. It is not rational,
yet it is not out of control, and best of all, it has an im-
measurably ancient right of entry into the world in which
logic has landed us defenceless, the world of ritual, magic
and religion, that world of darkness and candlelight which
Carroll declines to enter. We have seen already that Siva
is said to dice the world along; but it was Siva too who
danced the world into being, made and sustained and
redeemed it by his dancing. The cosmic dance is as old as
play, and older than Babylon. Everywhere dance is involved with ritual and poetry and religion, not merely in
paganism. High Mass has often been called a dance. In an

old poem Christ is heard entreating His true love to the dance, and Mr. C. S. Lewis[1] likens the Trinity to a dance in which all souls must share.

Poetry has its own fulness, its double balance and completion. Play too appears to have two sides; and if we have been playing one rather than the other in this book, because Nonsense seemed to be doing the same, we are none the less delivered finally to the other, not in spite of the logic but because of it. That is satisfying if rather alarming. It is no accident that children who are more logical than adults[2] are also so much more given to make-believe. Huizinga (*op. cit.*, Ch. I, p. 43) says that in what he calls holy play the child, the poet and the savage are all at home. Perhaps only these, if they are blessed and can escape the dangers of their playground, can know the fulness of play on both sides, the lovely skill and order and analysis, and this other, the make-believe and understanding by representation. Perhaps anyone who plays ought to experience both sides, as if it were not enough to be a bridge player without at the same time being a witch, or to be a chess expert without at the same time having a better understanding of the mysteries of God. Nonsense is a way into the first world, the reasonable side of play; but it must not be imagined that, just because this is rational activity, it will be understood, practised, taught in school. No one is taught it, at school or university—the managing of this side of the mind, in mathematics or logic or play or music or any constructional way of thinking. People do not know about it now, though one feels, from their curriculum, that the Middle Ages did. But Nonsense, as only a part of play, has performed its sisterly task and brought us to the other half, the irrational side of the mind with its entry into dream and magic and mystery. And no one teaches

[1] *Beyond Personality*, Geoffrey Bles, London, 1944, pp. 26–7.
[2] Cf. Jean Piaget, *The Language and Thought of the Child*, Harcourt Brace & Co., New York, 1926, p. 212, 'The child . . . conceives the world as more logical than it really is.'

this either, or knows about the connection between the two. They would laugh at the story of Albertus Magnus, St. Thomas' teacher and one of the great Scholastics, who besides being a master in mathematics and science was said to have an image in his room which bowed to him, saying '*Ave! Ave!*' as he went in and out. They teach one no magic at school, and one is lucky if one is still allowed any mystery in such religious instruction as may come one's way.

Both sides of the game need to be explained and thought about and taught. One could perhaps at least start to educate people on Nonsense and the dance, not regarding that as a programme for five-year-olds but for anyone who wants to have their minds working fully. It is so strange that it should be such new ground, for it is so old; only we have moved off it, so that Nonsense is thought to be a childish matter and we have forgotten the true nature of the dance. If someone could remind us, however, it would tell us something of this other half of ourselves which nobody educates now, so that it grows up in wild ignorance or sinks into atrophy, the dream half which is so enormously valuable if only it could be given a field of play such as that which Nonsense provides for our other half. Irrationally perhaps, one feels that dancing would be a way there, if one only knew how. And since it too is a kind of play, we could thus enlarge, according to our needs, the world of the mind we have found in Nonsense, and, not deserting the universe of bats and teatrays in the sky but taking it with us as a good and beloved if only partial share of our inheritance, move towards Babylon, that city of words, in the darkness under the star of a galliard.

BIBLIOGRAPHY

LEWIS CARROLL. *The Complete Works*. The Nonesuch Press, London, 1939.

EDWARD LEAR. *The Complete Nonsense*. Faber & Faber Ltd., London, 1947.

Letters. Edited by Lady Strachey. (2 vols.). T. Fisher Unwin, London, 1907.

Nursery Rhyme: *The Nursery Rhymes of England*, edited by James Halliwell, London, 1842.

*   *   *

ADLER, Mortimer J. *Dialectic*. Kegan Paul, Trench, Trubner & Co. Ltd., London, 1927.

AQUINAS, St. Thomas. *Summa Theologica*, Pts. I, I—II and II—II. Literally translated by Fathers of the English Dominican Province. Benziger Bros., Inc., New York, 1947.

ARISTOTLE. *Metaphysics, Poetics, Rhetoric*.

ARNOLD, Ethel M. *Reminiscences of Lewis Carroll, Atlantic Monthly*, June, 1929, p. 782.

AYRES, Harry Morgan. *Carroll's Alice*. Columbia University Press, New York, 1936.

BERGSON, Henri. *Laughter*: An Essay on the Meaning of the Comic. Translated by Cloudesley Brereton and Fred Rothwell. Macmillan Co., New York, 1921.

BINET, Alfred. *Psychologie des Grands Calculateurs et Joueurs d'Echecs*. Hachette et Cie, Paris, 1894.

BOREL, Emile, and CHERON, André. *Théorie Mathématique du Bridge:* à la Portée de Tous. Gauthier-Villars, Paris, 1940.

BOWEN, Wilbur P. *The Teaching of Play*. F. A. Bassette Co., Springfield, Mass., 1913.

BOWMAN, Isa. *The Story of Lewis Carroll*. J. M. Dent & Co., London, 1899.

CAMMAERTS, Emile. *The Poetry of Nonsense*. George Routledge & Sons Ltd., London, 1925.

CHÂTEAU, Jean. *Le Réel et l'Imaginaire dans le Jeu de l'Enfant*. J. Vrin, Paris, 1946.

CHESTERTON, G. K. *All Things Considered*. John Lane Co., New York, 1916.

As I Was Saying. Dodd Mead & Co., New York, 1936.

A Defence of Nonsense. (From *The Defendant*, 1901.) Included in *Selected English Essays*, edited by George G. Loane. Dent & Sons Ltd., London, undated.

Essay on Gilbert and Sullivan in *The Eighteen-Eighties*, edited by Walter De La Mare. Cambridge University Press, 1930.

The Victorian Age in Literature. Williams & Norgate, London, undated.

COLLINGWOOD, Stuart Dodgson. *The Life and Letters of Lewis Carroll*. T. Fisher Unwin, London, 1898.

CORIAT, Isador H. *The Meaning of Dreams*. Little, Brown & Co., Boston, 1920.

CULIN, Stewart. *Chess and Playing Cards*. Report of the U.S. National Museum for the year ending June 30th, 1896, pp. 679–942.

DAVIDSON, Angus. *Edward Lear: Landscape Painter and Nonsense Poet*. John Murray, London, 1938.

DE LA MARE, Walter. *Lewis Carroll*. Faber & Faber Ltd., London, 1932.

DE POSSEL, René. *Sur la Théorie Mathématique des Jeux de Hasard et de Réflexion*. Hermann et Cie, Paris, 1936.

EMPSON, William. *Some Versions of the Pastoral*. Chatto & Windus, London, 1935.

GROOS, Karl. *The Play of Man*. D. Appleton & Co., New York, 1901.

HARTLAND, Edwin Sidney. *The Science of Fairy Tales*. Walter Scott, London, 1891.

HASBROUCK, Muriel Bruce. *Pursuit of Destiny: with Thirty-Six Tarot Cards*. E. P. Dutton & Co. Inc., New York, 1941.

HAWKINS, D. J. B. *A Sketch of Mediæval Philosophy*. Sheed & Ward, New York, 1947.

HOLLINGWORTH, H. L. *The Psychology of Thought: approached through studies of sleeping and dreaming*. D. Appleton & Co., New York, 1927.

HUIZINGA, J. *Homo Ludens*. Pantheon Akademische Verlaganstalt, Amsterdam, 1939.

LANGER, Susanne K. *An Introduction to Symbolic Logic*. George Allen & Unwin Ltd., London, 1937.

LASKER, Emmanuel. *Common Sense in Chess*. J. S. Ogilvie Publishing Co., New York, 1895.

Manual of Chess. David McKay Co., Philadelphia, 1947.

LEE, Joseph. *Play in Education*. Macmillan Co., New York, 1921.

LENNON, Frances Becker. *Lewis Carroll*. Cassell & Co. Ltd., London, 1947.

MARITAIN, Jacques. *Art and Poetry*. Editions Poetry, London, 1945.
Art and Scholasticism, with other essays. Translated by J. F. Scanlan. Sheed & Ward, London, 1930.

MARSHALL, Frank J. *Comparative Chess*. David McKay Co., Philadelphia, 1932.

MASON, James. *The Art of Chess*. David McKay Co., Philadelphia, 1913.
The Principles of Chess: in Theory and Practice. Revised by Fred Reinfeld. David McKay Co., Philadelphia, 1946.

MEGROZ, R. L. *The Dream World: A Survey of the History and Mystery of Dreams*. John Lane, London, 1939.

MITCHELL, Edwin Valentine (Editor). *The Art of Chess Playing*. Barrows Mussey, New York, 1936.

MITCHELL, Elmer D., and MASON, Bernard S. *The Theory of Play*. A. S. Barnes & Co. Inc., New York, 1935.

MOSES, Belle. *Lewis Carroll in Wonderland and at Home: The Story of His Life*. D. Appleton & Co., New York and London, 1910.

ORWELL, George. *Shooting an Elephant and Other Essays*. Secker & Warburg, London, 1950.

PARTRIDGE, Eric. *Here, There and Everywhere: Essays upon Language*. Hamish Hamilton, London, 1950.

PIAGET, Jean. *Judgment and Reasoning in the Child*. Kegan Paul, Trench, Trubner & Co. Ltd., London, 1928.
The Language and Thought of the Child. Harcourt Brace & Co., New York, 1926.

READ, Carveth. *Man and His Superstitions*. Cambridge University Press, 1925.

REED, Langford. *The Life of Lewis Carroll*. W. & G. Foyle Ltd., London, 1932.

SACKVILLE-WEST, V. *Nursery Rhymes*. Michael Joseph, London, 1950.

SCHILLER, F. von. *Letters upon the Æsthetic Culture of Man*. Translated by J. Weiss. Little & Brown, Boston, 1845.

SCHORSCH, Robert S. *Psychology of Play*. Notre Dame, Indiana, 1942.

STEBBING, L. S. *A Modern Introduction to Logic*. Thomas Y. Cromwell Co., New York, 1930.

STILES, Percy Goldthwait. *Dreams*. Harvard University Press, 1927.

STRACHEY, Sir Edmund. *Nonsense as a Fine Art*. The *Quarterly Review*, 1888, p. 335.

STRONG, T. B. *Lewis Carroll. Cornhill Magazine*, 1898, p. 303.

TAINE, Hippolyte. *De l'Intelligence,* Tome Premier. Hachette, Paris, 1911 (12th edition).

TINDALL, W. Y. *James Joyce: His Way of Interpreting the Modern World.* Charles Scribner's Sons, New York and London, 1950.

VENN, John. *The Logic of Chance.* Macmillan & Co., London, 1876.

WALLAS, Graham. *The Art of Thought.* Harcourt Brace & Co., New York, 1926.

WHITEHEAD, Alfred North. *Essays in Science and Philosophy.* Philosophical Library, New York, 1947.

WOOD, Walter. *Children's Play: and its Place in Education.* Duffield & Co., New York, 1917.

WOOLF, Virginia. *The Moment and Other Essays.* Hogarth Press, London, 1947.

WOOLLCOTT, Alexander. *Introduction to Nonesuch Complete Works of Lewis Carroll* (q.v.).